# Wines
## OF NORTH AMERICA

# Wines
## OF NORTH AMERICA

CHARTWELL
BOOKS, INC.

First published in the United States of America by:
Chartwell Books Inc.
A Division of Book Sales Inc.
110 Enterprise Avenue
Secaucus, New Jersey 07094

Produced by Winchmore Publishing Services Limited
40 Triton Square
London NW1 3HG

Designed by Roy Williams
Maps by Pierre Tilley

ISBN 0-89009-627-9

Printed in Hong Kong

# Contents

# CHAPTER ONE
## Talking about Wines

If Puck, the mischievous sprite in *A Midsummer Night's Dream*, was a wine lover — which seems likely given his other name, Robin Goodfellow — we know where he would have put his girdle round the earth. It would have been a belt stretching roughly from latitude 37° North to 48° for it is in that strip that most of the world's wine is produced: certainly its best. (A similar belt almost equidistant from the Equator in the Southern Hemisphere includes the winegrowing areas of Australia, South America and South Africa.) Although the quality and character of wines depends on a variety of things — the grapes from which they are made, the soil on which they are grown, the skill of the maker, among other factors — all grapes and therefore vineyards demand certain climatic conditions. So it should come as no surprise that the vineyards and wineries of North America lie on the same latitudes as those of Europe. Those of California, for example, correspond closely with those of Spain and Italy; those of New York roughly with Bordeaux and Burgundy; those of Ontario, Canada roughly with the Champagne area of France.

It was the Romans, of course, who gave Europe, and particularly France, its historic lead in the production of wine. By the time they withdrew from Gaul after 500 years of occupation which began in 50 BC, the foundations of the present-day French wine industry had been well and truly laid and vineyards which existed then are still producing wine today. In later years the Church played its part in the development of wine production. The great religious institutions, such as the monasteries and abbeys, nearly all had their surrounding vineyards, often of considerable size. The Church lies behind the name of the popular Rhône wine, Châteauneuf-du-Pape. It was produced in the 14th century, as it is today, in the vineyards belonging to the first of the Avignon Popes, Clement V, who built a new château when he moved the papacy from Rome. Centuries later the Church played its part in the development of the wine industry in North America. As is described more fully later on, it was the Jesuit missions which first made wine in California in the 17th century and one variety of dark grape is still called the Mission grape. Similarly in Canada it was the Jesuits who first made wine, partly for sacramental purposes, partly for more selfish reasons. As late as 1872 the first Roman Catholic Bishop of Rochester, NY started what is now a flourishing commercial winery in

Previous page: Sterling's Diamond Mountain Vineyards in Napa Valley.

Right: Decorative fountain at the winery of the Château St Jean in Sonoma, California.

main wine producing areas

37°-48° latitudinal belts

New York State. During Prohibition many vineyards were able to keep going by making sacramental wine under permit.

So rapid is the development of the wine industry in the United States today that it is difficult to give up-to-date figures but some idea of their size can be obtained from the fact that in 1980 no less than 485,585,000 gallons of wine were produced – in 1981 some 50,000,000 less. Of this California produced about 90 percent.

When centuries ago the Roman legions advanced into Gaul there were no roads and progress was fastest along the river valleys. To protect themselves from hostile inhabitants they cleared the banks and lower slopes and later initiated the planting of vineyards on the cleared ground which proved highly suitable for viniculture. Thus many of the best-known European wines are associated with river valleys – the Rhine, the Rhône, the Loire, the Gironde, the Moselle etc. In North America the picture is much the same although for different reasons. In California there are the famous wineries of the Napa Valley, the not so well-known Russian River Valley, the Central Valley and the Salinas Valley. In upper New York State the vineyards are centered on the Finger Lakes, particularly on the shores of Keuka Lake and, also in New York there are vineyards in the Hudson River Valley. In Ohio vineyards on Bass

View of the Napa Valley, in California one of North America's most renowned wine-producing areas.

Early snow in the Boskydel Vineyards on Lake Leelanau, Michigan. Fortunately the grapes have been harvested.

Springtime at the Winery

Bully Hill® Vineyards

Estate Bottled
100% New York State

ROSÉ

Vintage 1981 Wine

Grapes and Wine Produced
and Bottled by the Estate Winery and Vineyard of
Bully Hill Vineyards, Inc.
Hammondsport, Steuben Co., New York 14840 U.
(607) 868-3610

Our products produced by the employees
of Bully Hill Vineyards, Inc. / Names upon

© 198

First Shuttle Flight
"COLUMBIA"
April 12, 1981

Cape Kennedy
Space Center

12% Alcohol
by Volume

BULLY HILL VINEYARDS® Vintage 1981
100% NEW YORK STATE

Space Shuttle Rose Wine
— SEMI-DRY —

Produced and Bottled by Bully Hill Vineyards, Inc.
Hammondsport, Steuben Co., New York, U.S.A. 14840
(607) 868-3610

and other islands in Lake Erie supply grapes to the wineries in Sandusky 20 miles away. In the south of the State of Silverton, near Cincinatti, a winery operates on the banks of the River Ohio.

The development of the North American wine industry has been closely associated with that of Europe. Many of the famous wineries in the United States were founded and developed by European experts and their names are commemorated on labels and in other forms today, for example, Fournier from France, Haraszthy of Hungary, the Gallos of Italy, Widmer from Switzerland and Beringer from Germany. The labels show a fine combination of the European and the native American tradition. Thus one could find a New York Chardonnay alongside Cold Duck (a blend of Champagne and sparkling Burgundy), a Cabernet Sauvignon alongside a Bully Hill Rosé, an Alexander Valley Gewürztraminer alongside a Hearty Burgundy, a Johannisberg Riesling alongside a Crackling Lake Niagara and so on. We should not be contemptuous of names which may seem outlandish to traditionalists. American wines have their own characteristics as do German, French and Italian. Some are very good indeed even if not up to the standard of the greatest wines of Burgundy or Bordeaux. However great wines are comparatively rare and good wines more common even in Europe. As someone once said, a great winemaker will make a great wine with fine grapes while an indifferent winemaker may still make a good wine with the same grapes. Or as a Californian summed it up pithily, 'In California we make the best California wines. In France they make the best French wines.'

It is not without reason that Leif Ericson called the part of North America he reached in about AD 1000 Vinland. The explorers found a plenitude of grapes. The basic principles of winemaking are the same wherever it is produced. The grapes are crushed when ripe, without breaking the seeds, and the juice allowed to ferment

Loading a press at the Hinzerling Vineyards. This small press is used to extract the *must*. Presses nowadays can be huge, pressing up to 50 tons of grapes in an hour.

helped by natural yeast. If it is white wine that is to be made, the skins of the grapes are removed before the juice goes into the vats to ferment. To make sweet white wine the fermentation is stopped while there is still sugar there: to make dry white wine fermentation is allowed to continue until the natural sugar is exhausted. An effervescent, fizzy wine is bottled before the completion of fermentation. For red wines the red or purple grape skins are left in the fermenting juice or *must* so that their color is absorbed. With rosé or pink wines the red skins are simply left in for a shorter time. These, it must be emphasized, are nothing but the basic principles. There is much more to winemaking, as will be explained later, but it can be seen that at this stage everything depends on the nature of the grape or grapes being used — their condition, ripeness, quality. It must be said that despite the plenitude of vines, the indigenous grapes of North America were not the best suited to winemaking, at least to European tastes and standards. They were the *vitis labrusca* and *vitis rotundifola* while the European grapes were *vitis vinifera*. Wines made from the American grapes tended to be sour or 'foxy' — some were, in fact, called fox-grapes. From time to time better varieties of indigenous grapes were developed by viticulturists, the Catawba and Concord being outstanding examples.

It was in the early part of the 19th century that a Frenchman with the significant name Jean-Louis Vigne, who was a cooper familiar with winegrowing and making, established a vineyard in California. He imported vine cuttings from Europe and thus did not have to use the traditional Mission grapes. Moreover he made his own casks from native oaks and thus became the first real commercial winegrower in the state. Few people awaiting their trains at Los Angeles Union Railroad Station today realize that they are standing on the site of his vineyard, El Aliso. Some 20 years later an even more significant figure in California wine history arrived in the state. This was

13

a Hungarian nobleman, Count Haraszthy. In 1857 he bought 560 acres of land in the Sonoma Valley and planted 80,000 vines and, a few years later, after visiting European vineyards he purchased some 200,000 vines consisting of 1,400 varieties which were brought into the state. Among them was probably the Zinfandel, thought to be a native Hungarian grape, whose wine is among the leading California products.

This intertwining of American and European grape relationships became even more pronounced. In the 1860s the disease phylloxera spread from the eastern United States not only to California but to Europe also. Phylloxera are small plant lice which suck the sap from the roots and leaves of the vines, stunting their growth and eventually killing them. The European wine industry was practically ruined by the disease with thousands of vineyards destroyed. Ironically although the vines of the eastern United States were responsible for the spread of the disease, the vines themselves had developed a resistance to it and the eventual solution was to graft the European vines onto an American root.

So just as vines in Europe have been strengthened by marriage to their trans-Atlantic cousins so have North American vines been refined by marriage to their longer established traditional European relatives. A glance at the list of grapes grown in the California vineyards makes this abundantly clear. We see, for example, the small tough-skinned grape Cabernet Sauvignon, foundation of the best wines from the Médoc vineyards near Bordeaux, France; or the purple Grenache, used in the making of Châteauneuf-du-Pape from the Rhône valley; or the green Chardonnay from which the famous white wines of Burgundy are made. They are by no means all French. There are, for example, the Traminer (or Gewürztraminer) of Alsace; the Sylvaner or Riesling of Germany; and the Barbera of Piedmont, Italy. We find the same thing in the New York State wineries. At the Vinifera Cellars at Hammondsport, which is run by one of North America's leading winemakers, Dr Konstantin Frank,

Right: Ripe Cabernet grapes at Sterling's Petersen Ranch, Napa Valley. They are used in the making of some of the best wines of Bordeaux, France and are now widely grown and used in North America.

Below: Old Zinfandel vine in San Jose at Mirassou, with the old Cribari winery in the background which is now used for barrel aging by the Mirassou Vineyards.

Bottom: Clos de Agoston, 'here is where it all began'. Sonoma Valley vineyard first planted by Count Agoston Haraszthy, one of California's first winemakers.

Beringer

ESTATE BOTTLED

1978

Napa Valley

Chardonnay

This private reserve Chardonnay was produced
exclusively from Chardonnay grapes grown on
the Beringer Estate Vineyards. The grapes were
picked at 24.7° Brix, 92 gm/100ml total acid.
The wine was aged for six months in Limousin
Oak. Grown, produced and bottled by Beringer
Vineyards, St. Helena, Napa Valley, California.
Alcohol 13.6% by volume.

Vines growing in the Napa Valley, California

not only do we find grapes of French and German origin but less-known varieties of grape such as the Hungarian Fetjaska that makes the best Russian champagne. The best quality wines, the premium wines, are usually but not always found among what are called the *varietals*. These are made entirely or for the most part from one grape whose name appears prominently on the label; for example, Beringer 1978 Napa Valley Chardonnay. The label shows where the grapes were grown, the temperature at which they were picked, length of aging etc. US Federal regulations require that 75 percent of the grapes used must come from the district named on the label – here Napa Valley – but California requires that in any wine labeled California 100 percent of the grapes must come from the state. Although the legal requirement is that only 51 percent of the named grapes in varietals has to be used, the best wineries use 75 percent or more and in California often 100 percent. It will be noted that the label illustrated states that the wine is made exclusively from Chardonnay grapes.

As has been said, winemaking was known as early as the 17th century in California and, indeed, in other parts of the United States. In Virginia as early as 1616 Lord De La Warr, the then Governor, had European vine cuttings sent over by the London Company. Efforts to establish viticulture continued on and off during the century in Massachussetts, Georgia, New York and the Carolinas but with little success. It was not until the first half of the 19th century that serious commercial wine production began and even then progress was uneasy. In California the annual vintage had reached 4,000,000 gallons by 1877 (to be quadrupled in the next 18 years) but some of the wine producers there had acquired a reputation for adulteration, mislabeling and other fraudulent activities so that a Pure Wine Law had to be passed in 1880 by the State legislature. Then came the setback of phylloxera and in 1920 the worst disaster of all, one that was shared by all the winemakers of the United States. This was Prohibition. Some vineyards were uprooted and given over to growing, of all things, prunes; some wineries sold off their winemaking equipment; some disappeared completely. The making of sacramental wine was not illegal so some wineries survived and a few enthusiasts kept their vineyards going out of sheer pride and determination. The 13 years of Prohibition brought the making of wine commercially to a standstill but it did not mean an end to winemaking. Indeed California grapes were shipped to the Eastern states where they were used in making home-made wine, the equivalent of bath-tub gin. There was one curious result from this. The amateur winemakers did not know much about the

Right: The rocky tunnels of the Beringer vineyards at St Helena, California used for aging and storing.

winemaking qualities of the different grapes and not unnaturally chose the largest and most splendid looking grapes which, unfortunately, did not always make the best wines. In fact during the 13 years of Prohibition the production of wine grapes in California actually doubled but, alas, they were not the best grapes for making fine wines.

Some wineries cheekily labeled their non-alcoholic wine products with warnings to customers that if they added yeast or other chemicals to the wine it would ferment and become alcoholic wine. One distinguished California winemaker makes no bones about what happened during the Prohibition years. The Trinchero family, owners of Sutter Home Winery at St Helena in the Napa Valley, arrived in the United States in 1920, at the height of Prohibition, and settled in New York City. They had been in the winemaking business in Italy for generations so they moved to upper New York State and opened what was euphemistically called an hotel resort but was in fact a speakeasy. There they bought grapes from California and made wine with which to regale their guests. There is little doubt that not a few vintners survived in similar ways.

However it is an ill wind that blows no one good. The setback of the Prohibition years meant that the wine industry could, as it were, start almost afresh, preserving what was best of the old practices and taking advantage of the best of the new, installing new equipment and benefiting from the latest scientific discoveries. The outcome was the great surge in the production of wine, much of it of high standard, that is still a feature of today. The maturing of vineyards is not a speedy process and the recovery from Prohibition is only now getting into full swing. It is remarkable that of some 50 wineries in New York State at least 20 began operation only in the last 11 years. A few, indeed, have not yet produced their first vintages, but all are engaged in the production of varietal wines. Similarly out of Michigan's 15 or so wineries nine date from 1970 or later. It is the same story in Washington State where at least 15 new wineries have sprung up during the same period. Of course there are wineries and wineries. The huge concern of E & J Gallo at Modesto in California buys grapes from some 100,000 acres of vineyards; the old-established firm of Beringer, also in California, has vineyards extending for 2,800 acres; in contrast the L Mawby Vineyards-Winery established in 1977 in Michigan extends for only 12 acres. The total acreage of vineyards (for wine) in the United States is estimated at up to 500,000 made up mainly as follows:

| California | 326,000 acres | Michigan | 17,000 acres |
|---|---|---|---|
| New York | 43,000 | Pennsylvania | 11,000 |
| Washington | 23,000 | Ohio | 4,000 |

These figures have increased rapidly in recent years and are likely to continue increasing. However what is vital for the expansion of wine production is the employment of new techniques in vinegrowing and winemaking.

The traditions associated with European wines are largely absent, but by no means entirely, from the American scene. Of course, some of the European traditions themselves do not stand up to close scrutiny. For instance the label designation 'Château bottled' only rarely means what it says for the 'château' is not likely to be the turreted castle of children's book but the modest building which is the center of the vineyard and its activities. European vinegrowing and winemaking usually take place on the same estate; however this is not always the case in the United States. For example one winery, that is where the wine is actually made, is situated in the industrial heart of Brooklyn, one of the five boroughs of New York City, where grapes grown in vineyards elsewhere in New York State are delivered in sterilized glass-lined tankers. The greatest difference especially with some of the more recently developed wineries lies in the modern equipment. The biggest winery in the world is E & J Gallo at Modesto in the San Joaquin or Central Valley of California. Gallos, as has been mentioned, uses the produce of 100,000 acres of vineyards throughout the state to produce wines ranging from the popular 'jug' varieties to good varietals and matured premium wines. The winery is capable of producing a fantastic 200,000,000 gallons and flying over Modesto one could be excused for confusing it with a huge

Top: The huge complex of the E & J Gallo Winery at Modesto, S California. It has a capacity of 200,000,000 gallons of wine.

Above: Modern pipeline 'switch-board' at the Great Western Winery in Hammondsport, New York.

oil depot in some Middle East port with its scores of stainless-steel tanks. It also contains the biggest glass bottle factory in the west of the United States, a striking contrast with the early days of wine in Southern California. Then, in the early 18th century, a German priest named Father Jorge Retz, lacking bottles and casks, actually stored wine in holes cut in the rocks and sealed with pitch. It is refreshing in more senses than one to imagine some latter-day Moses accidentally striking one of these reservoirs with his rod.

Most of what might be called wine language started, not surprisingly, in Europe but has now become international. However, as might be expected, North America has not only absorbed much of the international language but added some of its own. This short glossary will help readers:

**Aging**
The period during which wine is allowed to mature in barrels or bottles. Some fine table wines mature in oak barrels for years.

**Auslese**
A rich sweet wine made from selected very ripe grapes (Germany).

**Apéritif wine**
A wine served as an appetizer before a meal, for example, sherry.

**Body**
The consistency of a wine partly related to alcoholic and tannic content. Wines may be described as light, medium or full.

**Bouquet**
Not a bunch of flowers but the fragrance of the wine when the bottle is opened.

## Breathing
The process of allowing air to reach the wine by drawing the cork or decanting.

## Brix
A measurement by weight of the sugar content of grapes on maturity.

## Brut
Used to describe very dry Champagne in France and sometimes in North America.

## Chambrer
The French word for the process of bringing red wine up to the temperature of the room in which it is being served.

## Champagne
The sparkling white wine made in the Champagne area of France and in North America by the *méthode Champenoise*. The French do not like the American version to be called Champagne and under US law it must be described as coming from a given area but it is still called Champagne. The *méthode Champenoise* involves a second fermentation and trapping the gases in the bottle. (See also Charmat process and Remuage.)

## Charmat process
A method of making Champagne by bulk fermentation.

## Château bottled or 'Mise en bouteille au Château'
Often seen on French wine labels it may really mean only that the wine was bottled where it was made, sometimes, it is true, in a château, but more often in a more modest building in the vineyard. The nearest North American equivalent is 'estate bottled' and is generally used only when winery and vineyard are closely associated in the same area.

## Color
Whether red or white the color of a wine is a strong indication of its quality. If it is cloudy it is suspect, if clear and bright reassuring. Not for nothing does the name 'claret' come from the French word for clear.

## Decanting
The process of emptying the wine from the bottle into a special container or decanter, allowing any sediment to remain in the bottle and permitting the wine to breathe.

Previous page: Greystones, on the northern outskirts of St Helena, California, where the Christian Brothers make their Champagne and age their premium wines.
Inset: Concannon, a North American château in Livermore Valley.

Left: Wine tasting at Sonoma County Harvest Fair (l to r: Craig Goldwyn, Chuck Chapman, Leon Adams, Andre Tchelistcheff and Dr Vern Singleton).

Below: A Napa Valley wine auction with Michael Broadbent presiding.

### Dry
A description of wine which, because most of its sugar content has been changed into alcohol by fermentation, is lacking in sweetness.

### Fortified wine
This is a wine which has been strengthened by the addition of brandy — for example, port and sherry. The alcohol content is thus increased to anything between 14 percent and 18 percent.

### Foxy
A strong, somewhat disagreeable aroma and taste associated with many native North American grapes (known as fox-grapes) and consequently with wine made wholly from them.

### Generic wines
These are wines named after European producing areas, the names being permitted by US law to be used but always with the actual place of origin also stated — for example, California Port. They are: Burgundy, Claret, Chablis, Champagne, Chianti, Hock, Malaga, Madeira, Moselle, Port, Rhine Wine, Sauterne, Sherry, Tokay.

### Hybrid grapes
Grapes which result from the crossing of native American grapes, with their resistance to phylloxera, with European grapes which help to make finer wines.

### Jug wines
Very much the *vin ordinaire* of the United States, so called because they are often sold in gallon or half gallon containers.

### Kabinett
The lowest rating in German quality wines.

### Must
The result of crushing grapes for their juice in the first stages of winemaking.

### Noble rot
English translation of the French term (*pourriture noble*) for *botrytis cinerea*, a fungus which attacks some grapes, dehydrating them with a resulting excessive sweetness.

### Premium
The description used in the United States for high-quality wine.

### Remuage
The regular twisting/shaking of Champagne bottles to dislodge the sediment during aging — a feature of the *méthode Champenoise*.

### Rosé
A pink wine obtained by reducing the period during which red grape skins are allowed to ferment in the must.

### Tannin
An ingredient of grape skins which provides an agreeable astringency in wine and also helps to produce clarity and brightness.

### Tawny
Usually applied to Port and other red wines which through long maturing have lost their redness and become brownish in color.

### Varietal
A premium wine in the United States made predominantly or entirely from the grape variety named on the label.

### Vineyard
The land on which grapes are grown. In Europe the making of the wine is usually done at the vineyard: in North America it can be and often is made elsewhere.

### Winery
The place where the wine is actually made.

# CHAPTER TWO

## Winemaking

As the previous chapter suggests, despite the close links that developed between wine production in Europe and North America, the wine scenes in the two differ in many fundamental aspects. In France, for example, when we speak of a Burgundy, a Médoc, a Rhône wine we are speaking in general terms of a certain type of wine produced in a certain area. In modern North American wine language the description attached relates to the particular grape used. Thus we have the same wine names in states as far apart as California and New York. The wine drinker who enjoys his white Chablis or Pouilly-Fuissé in all likelihood does not know, nor indeed need to know, that they are made from the Chardonnay grape. The lover of the clarets of St Emilion probably does not know that they are made from the Cabernet Sauvignon and Merlot grapes, or that Beaujolais owes its flavor to the Gamay grape. Under the French *appellation controlée* system a wine labeled St Emilion, for example, must come from that small area near Bordeaux which includes the small town and commune of St Emilion itself. Six associated communes as it happens are also entitled to use the appellation but only combined with the name of the commune. They are Lussac St Emilion, Montagne St Emilion, Parsac St Emilion, Puisseguin St Emilion, Sables St Emilion and St Georges St Emilion. The whole area covers little more than a couple of dozen square miles. In the United States with the recent development of varietals Cabernet Sauvignon grapes are widely grown and used to make wines in states as widely separated as California, Idaho, New York and Michigan. As has been said wines owe their individual characteristics not just to the quality of the grape used but to the soil and climate in which they are grown and picked, and to the skill of the winemakers in fermenting, pressing, aging, bottling etc. It is clear, therefore, that the variations in North American Cabernet Sauvignon wines, to take one example, are likely to be far greater than those from the restricted area of St Emilion.

Very much the same applies to the Chardonnay grape and champagne. In France production of champagne is confined to the Champagne country covering about 58,000 acres. In North America every wine state produces Chardonnay wine under one name or another, often actually calling it Champagne or describing it as being made by the *méthode Champenoise*. Thus, whereas the typical European vineyard or

Previous page: Harvesting grapes in Canada. Canada has a small but flourishing and growing wine industry, centered largely in Ontario.

1980
Estate Grown

Hargrave Vineyard
North Fork
Long Island
New York
Merlot
Table Wine Produced & Bottled By Hargrave Vineyard
Cutchogue, N.Y.

A vineyard in the Napa Valley, California prepared for fumigation prior to planting.

Rows of vines on the Weibel Vineyards of Mission San Jose, California. This Champagne-producing winery has been in existence since 1939.

winery produces wines identifiable with that area, in North America wineries produce a wide variety of wines with as wide a range of characteristics. Moreover wines are as often as not made from grapes not grown in the area at all. New York champagne, for example, may be made from Chardonnay grapes grown in the kinder climate of California.

This use of grapes grown elsewhere may result in any given winery producing wines of bewildering variety. It is here that the soil and climate and particularly the skill of the winemaker come very much into the picture. Modern American winemakers are fond of referring to 'microclimates.' By this they mean special climatic conditions not enjoyed by the surrounding areas but found in small pockets. It is another way of saying that because you do not expect to be able to grow certain grapes in Ohio with its harsh winter conditions there are nevertheless certain small areas in the state where they will flourish, because of the lie of the land, or the effect of nearby lakes on temperature, which affects early or late frosts, or other factors. Many home gardeners are familiar with this phenomenon, discovering that some plants which have difficulty in surviving in one part of the garden will flourish in another. Even California, generally thought of as one great sun bath, has its microclimates with some grapes succeeding in one place but not in another.

We have described the basic principles of winemaking but the process of making quality wines is a good deal more complicated than that description implies. The skill of the winemaker brings out the virtue in the grapes. As has been described the first stage consists of crushing the grapes and skins, but not the stalks, to make the must which is then allowed to ferment in vats through the actions of yeasts. Grape skins actually have on them a number of organisms including yeast but often pure yeast is added to the must by the winemaker and the choice of specific yeast strains is important. This is not the place for a detailed scientific description of the processes involved and in general terms it is sufficient to say that in the must the yeast cells

Above: A lone vine stands silent vigil over sloping acres of choice wine variety grapes in a California vineyard.

Below: A rich green vineyard stretching off toward the distant mountains of a California wine district.

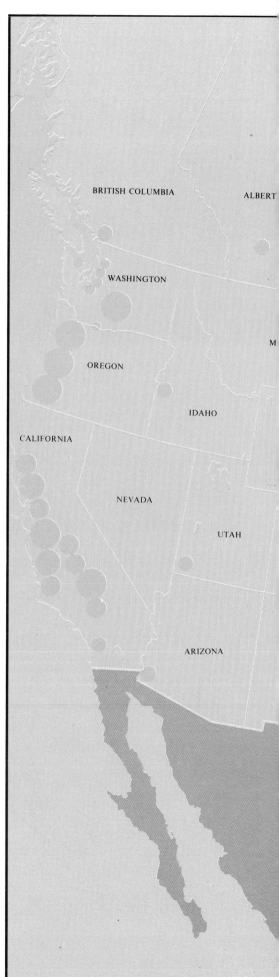

BRITISH COLUMBIA

ALBERT

WASHINGTON

M

OREGON

IDAHO

CALIFORNIA

NEVADA

UTAH

ARIZONA

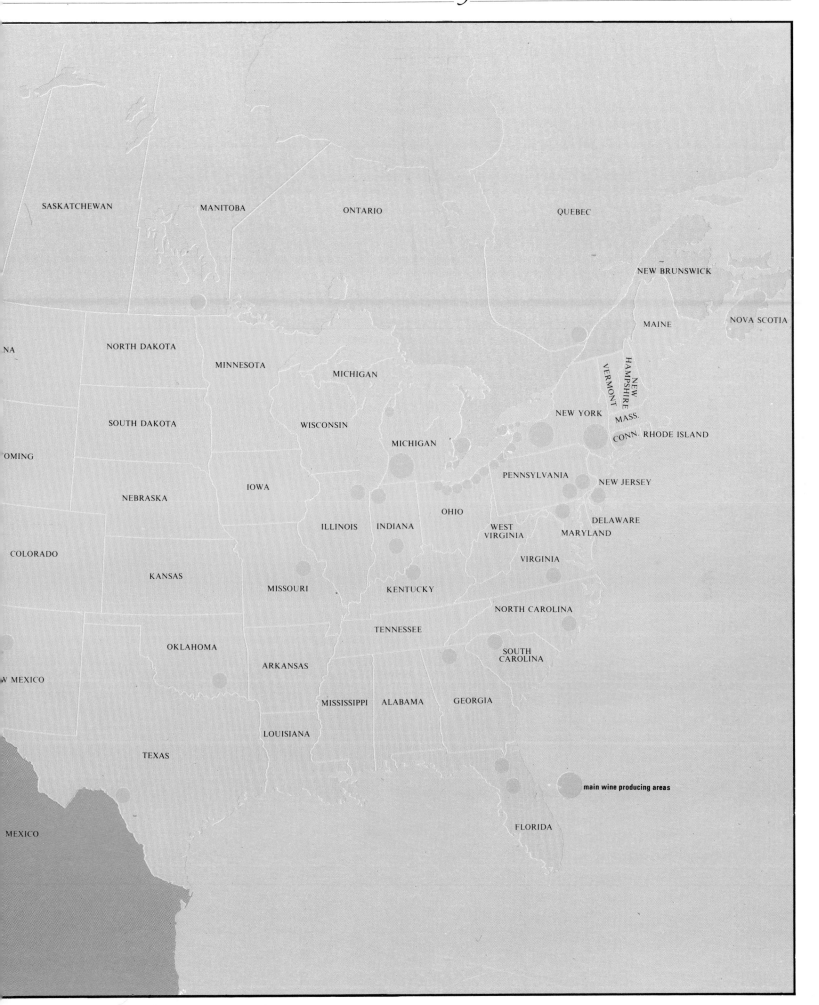

SASKATCHEWAN
MANITOBA
ONTARIO
QUEBEC

NEW BRUNSWICK

MAINE
NOVA SCOTIA

NORTH DAKOTA
MINNESOTA
MICHIGAN

NEW HAMPSHIRE
VERMONT

SOUTH DAKOTA
WISCONSIN
NEW YORK
MASS.
CONN. RHODE ISLAND

MICHIGAN

PENNSYLVANIA
NEW JERSEY

IOWA
OHIO
DELAWARE

NEBRASKA
ILLINOIS
INDIANA
WEST
VIRGINIA
MARYLAND

COLORADO
VIRGINIA

KANSAS
MISSOURI
KENTUCKY

NORTH CAROLINA

TENNESSEE

OKLAHOMA
SOUTH
CAROLINA

ARKANSAS

NEW MEXICO
MISSISSIPPI
ALABAMA
GEORGIA

LOUISIANA

TEXAS

main wine producing areas

MEXICO
FLORIDA

NORTH DAKOTA

WYOMING

NA

multiply and in doing so turn the sugar in the must into alcohol and carbon dioxide with a very small portion also of glycerine and a substance called succinic acid. The last two help produce the softness of the wine but the proportion of them is tiny — less than four percent of the whole, the yield of alcohol and carbon dioxide being about 95 percent divided roughly between the two. The quicker the yeast works the better the fermentation that takes place so the skilled winemaker finds ways of speeding it up, particularly by the addition of sulphur dioxide. This is a highly delicate operation for too much can have the opposite effect of that desired as well as harming both the bouquet and body of the wine. Traditionally fermentation took place in oak barrels but today in modern wineries it is in stainless steel or glass-lined vats although many winemakers insist that the old method adds quality to the wine, particularly red varieties.

The first fermentation, during which the temperature of the must rises considerably has to be carefully watched, and usually takes up to about 10 days but can be much longer. The desirable temperature is important and varies between white and red wines with the must for white wines kept at below 18°C and for red perhaps half as hot again. With the completion of the first fermentation, that is when only a small quantity of sugar remains in the must, the wine is drawn off leaving a saturated residue called pomace. The next stage is to crush or press this pomace thus producing more wine to be added to that already drawn off. To make most white wines this pressing takes place before fermentation, something which raises a special problem with yeast and the special strains to be added.

Above: The Modern: stainless-steel storage tanks at Masson's famous Pinnacles Vineyard in Monterey county.

Right: The Traditional: aging vats at the Pinnacles Vineyard.

30

After pressing comes fining and racking or clarification of the wine. This is done by adding a clarification agent such as egg white or isinglass causing any solids to sink to the bottom when the wine can be drawn off. Then the winemaker must reach the decision on how long each individual wine needs to be aged. This may be in oak barrels or casks, or in stainless-steel or glass containers before being bottled. Many premium wines continue aging in the bottle.

It is obvious from all this that however good the soil, however kind the weather and however fine the grape it is the skill of the winemaker in the final stages that may label the wine good, bad or indifferent. Many American wine labels indicate the alcoholic strength of the wine, ranging from about seven percent for lighter table wines to 18 percent for fortified wines. It should be remembered that some wines attain a high alcoholic degree naturally, for example the wines of the Rhône valley in France, but fortified wines such as port and sherry achieve it unnaturally as it were by the addition of brandy at some stage.

Let us now take a look at the basis of it all – the grape. Vineyards tend to thrive in similar topographical conditions, that is, on rocky or gravelly soil close to rivers or

Above: Vines are partial to rocky soil and frequently vineyards have to the layman a deceptive appearance of neglect.

Right: The dust and cobwebs of ages in the storage tunnels of the Beringer Vineyards in California.

Spraying the vines in Canada.

Pruning vines at the Concannon Vineyards in the Livermore Valley.

lakes — in Europe and in North America. It takes a long time after planting before vineyards begin to yield their harvest. The first four or five years are spent in the creation of the vine's deep root system and developing a strong woody stock. The gravelly soil typical of good vinegrowing areas allows drainage for rain water and the vine roots dig deep to reach it. In doing so they absorb minerals which contribute to the quality of the fruit. If nature were allowed to take its course the plant, once the roots were established, would run riot pushing out the long branches typical of vines and creepers. It is here that the viticulturist steps in with his knife and secateurs, pruning the vines back almost to the main stem in midwinter. In spring, as early as April in places, young shoots appear from the coarse wood of the vine and rapidly turn to stalks and leaves with flowers appearing soon after. This is a danger period for late frosts can easily destroy the young growths. This is when microclimates come into play and some viticulturists resort to artificial means of heating or rather warming their vineyards. Sometimes this is done by large flame throwers directed over the vines. Once the danger of late frost is safely passed, heavy summer rain or hail is the next danger, but all being well by June the grapes can be seen and by August have set and are well on the way to ripening. Harvesting takes place in September or October but here again early frosts present a threat. Most harvesting, at least on smaller size vineyards, is still done by hand (incidentally providing seasonal labor) with small shears or knives used to cut the grape bunches, but mechanical harvesters are by no means unknown, sometimes with the grapes being crushed on the harvester and the juice pumped into an accompanying tanker.

Top left: Most grapes for winemaking are still picked by hand but the use of mechanical harvesters, top right, (seen here in Canada)

Sometimes, when the grapes have suffered from too little heat and sunshine their sugar content is insufficient to produce the right amount of alcohol during fermentation. On average the sugar content of the grape juice should be about 20 percent, nearly 80 percent being water with very small percentages of acids, mineral salts etc. As a rule of thumb two degrees of sugar in the grape juice would be expected to yield one degree of alcohol so, as can be imagined, the winemaker's first thought is of the sugar content of his grape juice. As the grapes ripen the sugar content gets higher and the acid content lower and it is up to the winemaker (with the aid of a saccharometer) to choose the crucial moment. Of course grapes have their individual characteristics but the best point seems to be from 20 percent to 23 percent sugar content. Where there is a deficiency winemakers may resort to a process called chaptalization, adding sugar to the must during fermentation. It is an operation of some delicacy because adding too much while increasing the alcohol content may well spoil the character of the wine and it is consequently frowned upon in some quarters. Chaptalization is useful in wineries in colder climates but usually unnecessary in hotter climates and, indeed, is forbidden in Italy, for example. In any case adding more than about two percent is regarded as undesirable.

A small but not unimportant part of the grape juice is made up by two acids — tartaric and malic. Generally speaking the acid content is higher in cool climates, lower in hot so in the eastern part of the United States the acidity is usually on the high side while in California it is lower. Here again the skill of the winemaker comes into play with the delicate operation of controlling the acid content.

is growing, especially in larger vineyards. Above: The picked grapes of the Martini Vineyards are loaded into a stemmer-crusher.

## GRAPES

As the English poetess Elizabeth Barrett Browning wrote, with a discernment not usually attributed to the ladies of the period, 'The wine must taste of its own grapes.' As has been said it is the flavor and quality given by the grape or grapes which provide the basis of every wine however skilled and imaginative the maker. Here is a list of the principal varieties, native American or European in origin, used by North American wineries. There are others but these are the chief varieties.

### Aurora
A Franco-American hybrid used in making white wines.

### Baco Noir
A hybrid grape used either by itself or with other grapes to produce a dark red table wine.

### Barbera
A red grape with high alcoholic content originating in Piedmont, Italy. In the United States grown mainly in the warm San Joaquin Valley of California. Ages well.

### Cabernet Sauvignon
Not the handsomest of grapes, being small and coarse-skinned and blue-green in color, but famous for making some of the best Bordeaux wines. The wine has a good fragrance, is dry and long-lasting.

### Catawba
Probably the best known of the native American wine grapes developed in the early 19th century and popular until Prohibition. Purple, it was an accidental cross of *vitis labrusca*, producing white or pale red wine rather 'foxy' in flavor.

### Chancellor Noir
A Franco-American hybrid used in making white wine.

### Chardonnay
A pale green grape which produces some of the world's finest dry white wines such as those of Burgundy, for example, Chablis, Montrachet, and Champagne. In California it produces well-perfumed wine of character.

### Chelois
A Franco-American hybrid used in making red wines.

### Chenin Blanc
A golden white grape used in the wines of Anjou and Touraine in France, such as Vouvray, and the basis of dry, sweet and sparkling white wines in California where it is sometimes wrongly called Pinot Blanc.

Far left: Seyval Blanc grapes of the Boskydel Vineyards nearing maturity.

Left: Pinot Chardonnay grapes.

**Concord**

A strong but small native North American grape of the *vitis labrusca* family grown as much to be eaten as made into wine. It makes a strong dark wine and is often used in Kosher wine.

**Delaware**

A pink native American grape made into a distinctive white wine.

**Dutchess**

A native North American grape used in making white wines.

**Gamay**

The pale purple grape from which Beaujolais is made in France and which has the unique quality of producing somewhat indifferent wine elsewhere. It is used to produce a vin rosé in California.

**Gewürztraminer**

A golden, early ripening grape best known in Alsace and in Germany producing a white wine with a strong bouquet and flavor. Used widely in California.

**Grenache**

A sweet purple grape from the Rhône Valley in France where it is used to make Châteauneuf-du-Pape, also Tavel, the Rhône vin rosé. In California it is used successfully in vin rosé and dry white wine.

**Ives**

A native North American grape used in making white wine.

**Maréchal Foch**

A Franco-American hybrid used in making red wine.

**Merlot**

With the Cabernet Sauvignon, the other great grape of the Bordeaux area and also used in making St Emilion and Pomerol, this grape is achieving considerable popularity in North America.

**Muller-Thurgau**

A cross-breed of Riesling.

**Muscat**

One of the earliest of the wine grapes producing intensely sweet wine such as Muscadet.

**Niagara**

A native American grape originating in the Niagara Peninsula and used in making a rather 'foxy' sweet white wine.

**Pinot Noir**

This famous red grape of the Côte d'Or wines of Burgundy such as Chambertin, Corton and Musigny, is also used in making Champagne and some German red wines. A Pinot Noir from the small Eyrie Vineyard in McMinnville, Oregon, achieved the distinction of coming second (to a Chambolle-Musigny) in a blind tasting in Beaune, France in 1980.

**Riesling (white) or Johannisberg Riesling**

A late ripening German grape used in making Rhine and Moselle wines and dry white and dessert wines in many parts of the United States.

**Scuppernong**

A native North American grape used in making white wine.

**Seibel**

The name of a number of varieties of red wine grapes hybridized by an early French vintner named Seibel

**Sémillon**

A grape used with Sauvignon in making the dry Graves and the sweet Sauternes of Bordeaux, France. On the sweet side it is liable to be attacked by the 'noble rot' (*botrytis cinerea*), an overripening which concentrates sugar and flavor leading to

Cabernet Sauvignon grapes.

fine sweet wine.

### Seyval Blanc
Like Seibel, varieties of grape hybridized by a contemporary Frenchman named Seyve-Villard.

### Sylvaner
A German white grape somewhat similar to Riesling but with less acidity, often called Riesling in California.

### Syrah (sometimes Shiraz) or Petite Sirah
Another variety of grape from the Rhône Valley of France. Dark colored, the wine has a strong bouquet and needs aging.

### Zinfandel
A grape thought to be of Hungarian origin and highly successful in California in producing red wing.

## CHAMPAGNE

Special mention has to be made of the making of Champagne which differs considerably from the normal process of winemaking previously described. The *méthode Champenoise* – the way they do it in France – has made the Champagne district in northern France, with its center the cathedral city of Rheims, famous for what is undoubtedly the best known wine by name in the world. The grapes used are usually a blend of Pinot Noir and Chardonnay in an approximate proportion of two to one respectively. The Pinot Noir is, as its name indicates, a dark grape and is perhaps the best grape of all for making fine red wines. Champagne is a white wine so the first problem is to ensure that the Pinot Noir grapes are quickly pressed after picking and are unbruised so that the juice produced by the pressing is white and not pink. For this reason great care is exercised not only in the selection but in the handling of the grapes. In its first stages the making of Champagne is the same as making any still white wine. The must of the *cuvée*, the first drawing off from the pressing and therefore the best grape juice, is allowed to ferment and stand for some eight to 10 weeks when it should be completely dry, that is, all or nearly all of its sugar content will have become alcohol. It is then racked and at this stage the all-important blending of the different cuvées takes place. The new wine then stands for another month or more allowing for further fermentation and is racked again so that bottling

An aerial view of the Weibel Champagne vineyards.

Top: Oak casks of aging Champagne.

Above: Champagne bottles, neck down ready for the remuage in the limestone cellars of the Mon Ami Champagne Company, Ohio.

Above right: Bottling machine at Mon Ami, which prides itself on employing the *méthode Champenoise.*

can take place in about April of the year following that of the grape harvest.

At the bottling stage a small quantity of what is called *liqueur de tirage* is dissolved in the wine. This consists of sugared champagne wine with perhaps a yeast starter, whose effect, during the fermentation that follows in the bottle, is to create carbonic acid gas, thus providing the bubbly element. Champagne bottles are made extra strong because of the pressure created by the gas which is retained in the bottle, the cork being firmly wired on to resist the pressure. The bottles are then laid on their sides, sometimes in stacks 20 bottles high in the cool tunnels of the Champagne country chalk hillsides where slow fermentation takes place for three or four months and sometimes even years. During this period a sediment forms and has to be removed. The first stage in this is the *remuage*, an operation still performed by hand, in which each bottle, neck down, is briskly twisted causing the sediment to dislodge

and slide down the bottle to rest on the bottom of the cork. Later comes the delicate operation of removing the sediment from the bottle losing only a minimum of wine and gas. This takes place after frequent *remuages* and is called the *dégorgement*. It involves removing or dislodging the cork so that the sediment follows in the expulsion of gas and is achieved by freezing the bottle neck in one way or another to form a small ice block attached to the cork and the sediment. When the cork is removed it takes with it the ice block. The gas being cold not much wine is lost and is anyhow replaced by what is called the *liqueur d'éxpedition* which is added quickly before the bottle is finally corked. This is a mixture of sugar, still champagne and brandy and finally controls the degree of sweetness to be given to the wine. The bottle is then corked with the familiar mushroom-shaped cork which is wired to the neck of the bottle. All that remains is to finish off the bottle (in more senses than one) but at this stage with labels and bright foil covering the cork.

That, briefly explained, is the *méthode Champenoise* and given the complicated nature of the process goes some way to explain the cost of this celebration wine. There is another way of making Champagne, known as the Charmat process, which involves bulk fermentation in sealed containers. It is used by some North American winemakers of repute but it is not the *méthode Champenoise* and the French, who object to wines produced outside the Champagne country of France being called Champagne anyhow, may be entitled to object even more when it is not even made by their *méthode*.

## FORTIFIED WINES

### Sherry

The wine takes its name from the town of Jerez de la Frontera, about 15 miles inland from Cadiz in Spain. It is a fortified wine because after fermentation grape spirit is added and a further process, the *solera* system, follows to determine the category of

the wine. There are, in fact, four main categories: Amontillado, Fino, Manzanilla and Oloroso. Amontillado is darkish and slightly sweet; Fino pale in color and dry in character; Manzanilla, from the coastal area around Sanlucar de Barrameda, about 20 miles from Jerez de la Frontera, fine and dry with a slightly salty flavor; Oloroso is darker and as sold usually sweeter although, in fact, it is a dry wine to begin with. When the wine is made the must is fermented as usual but is not racked, being allowed to stand around in special butts which allow oxygen to reach the wine, for two or three months. During this time and later a mold, characteristic of sherry and known as *flor*, forms on the top. In January the wine is racked and given the first fortification of grape spirit, a little less than two percent is added and the wine again allowed to stand for as long as a year or more before being racked and going through the *solera* process of blending. Briefly this consists of drawing off some of the oldest wine and progressively topping up each wine with a younger similar one. Not many North American wineries use the *solera* system but seek a sherry effect by aging in heat and the 'sherries' they produce, say the purists, are not really sherries at all. The grapes usually used for producing sherry are Palomino and Pedro Ximenes and both of these grow well in California.

### Port

This fortified wine takes its name, of course, from Oporto in Portugal and the grapes from which it is made are grown in the terraced vineyards on the steep rocky slopes of the banks of the River Douro. It is best known as a red wine but white port has a considerable following. Port is essentially a blended wine and is made from a considerable variety of grapes, mostly thick-skinned, which accounts for the deep red color of the wine. The grapes are crushed in shallow containers and the must allowed to ferment until the sugar content has been reduced to about 10 percent. At this stage fermentation is stopped by drawing the wine off into casks which already contain sufficient brandy to bring the fermentation to a halt. The wine is then taken down to Oporto where it is blended and stored in pipes (a special long cask peculiar to port) in warehouses known as lodges sometimes for decades and usually for some years. Types of Port are: Ruby, young and red and aged for two years; Tawny, matured in the wood for many years, it fades to a tawny color; Crusted, a blend of high quality wine of different years so called because of the light deposit which forms in the bottle; and Vintage Port which is wine of an outstanding year matured for two years in the wood and perhaps 20 or more in the bottle. As with sherry the purists do not believe that the Ports made in North America are true ports as they are not made from the wide variety of grapes which allow for blending.

### BRANDY

It is true that brandy is not a wine but its basis is the grape and therefore deserves some consideration in any book on wines. In fact it could be said that brandy is white wine with most of the liquid removed. This is achieved by distillation, a process which, put very simply, means heating the wine to produce a vapor which is then condensed to produce the spirit. That is putting it very simply indeed for any cognac drinker knows that there are very good and very bad brandies so it cannot be just a question of boiling up the wine and condensing the steam. It begins, of course, with the grape. In France they use mainly the Ugni Blanc, often picked before they are ripe to ensure plenty of acidity. In the winter as soon as the wine has fermented distillation begins. Ten gallons of wine may be expected to produce about one of brandy. The wine is slowly heated and rises in the form of vapor to pass through a coiled copper pipe which is cooled causing the vapor to condense. The first spirit condensed is not used for cognac, the second, containing something like 70 percent aldohol, is. It is then matured in oak barrels for a minimum of two years, usually between two and five, though it can be for 30 to 40 years. Sugar or caramel may be used to regulate sweetness and normally the alcoholic content is brought down to about 40 percent by the addition of distilled water.

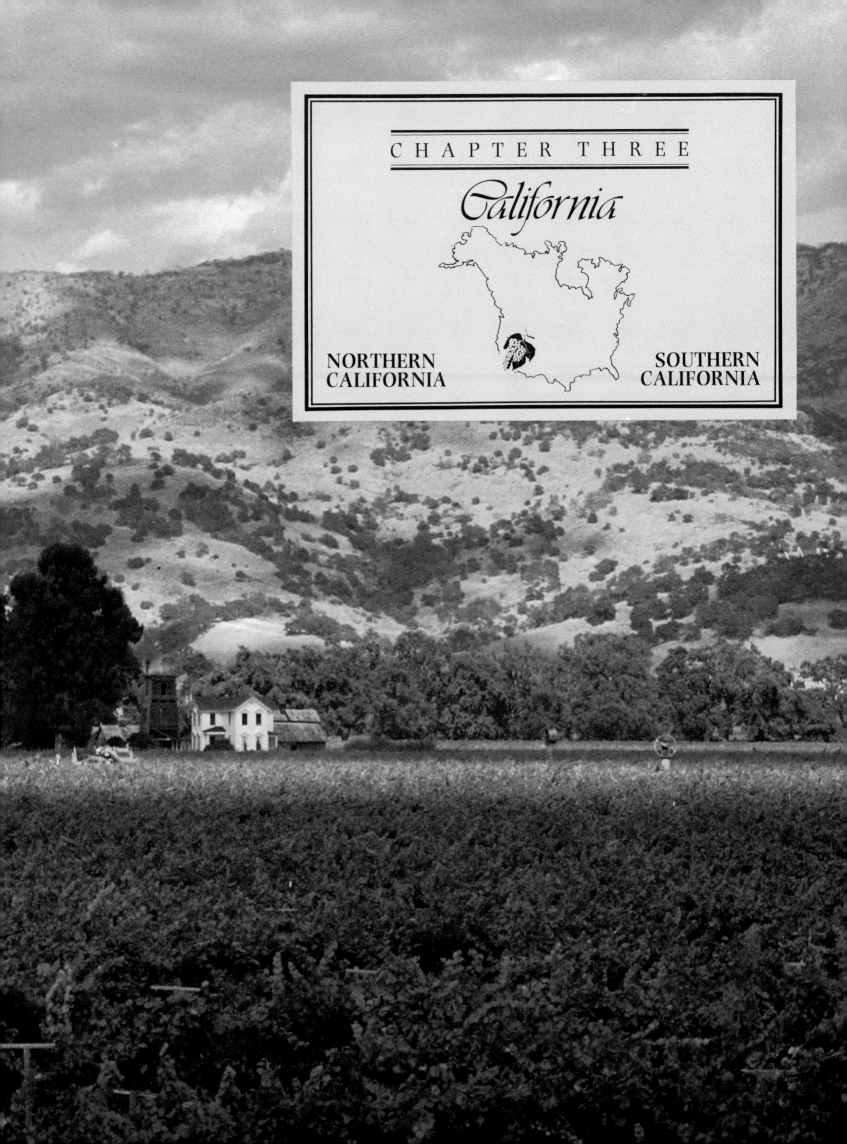

# CHAPTER THREE

## *California*

**NORTHERN CALIFORNIA**                    **SOUTHERN CALIFORNIA**

The Jesuit missions began California's long history of viniculture in Lower California at the end of the 17th century. It should be remembered that California was until 1822, a Spanish colony, part of Mexico. Then Mexico won its independence from Spain and became a republic so that California was a Mexican province. It remained one until the middle of the century when the United States won the Mexican war of 1846–47. In fact California became the 31st state of the Union only in 1850. So the early history of the development of California as a wine-producing area falls into three broad periods — that under Spanish rule when it seems to have been mainly an affair of the Jesuit missions. The second period was under Mexico when foreigners such as Joseph Chapman, an American, Jean-Louis Vigne of France, John Sutter, a Swiss, and others planted vineyards further north. The last phase was in the decades from the 1850s on when development proceeded apace. The new American state welcomed newcomers, particularly after the Civil War ended in 1865 when thousands of settlers moved across to the West. Moreover the huge influx of immigrants from Europe between 1840 and 1860 to the United States must have brought with it a demand for wine, their traditional drink. By the 1860s the Sonoma Valley, where Count Haraszthy had developed his vineyard and winery of Buena Vista, was beginning to flourish and in the nearby Napa Valley the Prussian Charles Krug and his cellarmaster Jacob Beringer were establishing their reputations.

Under Spanish rule winemaking was principally conducted by the Jesuit fathers. It is known that in 1697 one of them, Father Juan Ugarte, planted a vineyard of sorts to make wine for his mission of Saint Francis-Xavier in Lower California and another vineyard was planted in another mission further north 11 years later. The missions were to spread steadily to the north under the leadership of a Franciscan, Father Junipero Serra, whose statue stands in Los Angeles and whose Christian name brings to mind gin rather than wine. Each mission had its church, orchards and vineyards and most of them were on sites where California's modern cities such as San Diego and Los Angeles would grow. By the end of the 18th century, as the territory was developed, privately owned vineyards appeared alongside those of the missions and began slowly to replace them. Indeed after the independence of Mexico the missions were taken over by the State and their vineyards were to disappear. One priest, Padre Vicente Sarria of the Mision de Nuestra Senora de la Soledad, who refused to leave, actually died of starvation on the altar steps. It was in the 1820s and 1830s that Chapman, Vigne and others gave the winemaking industry fresh impetus so that when California joined the Union in 1850 it was already producing considerable quantities of wine and what is more selling them. By then the wine industry was developing rapidly in the two areas north of San Francisco which are now world renowned — the Sonoma and Napa Valleys — and even the Russians who had a fur-trading post in Sonoma County planted vines.

It was in 1849 that Count Agostan Haraszthy de Mokesa, a noble refugee from the Austro-Hungarian Empire, arrived in California. He had already been in the United States, in Wisconsin, for nine years but had not concerned himself much with wine, except presumably as a consumer. His arrival in California, where he moved for health reasons, was to revolutionize the wine scene. He quickly planted vineyards, importing vines from Hungary, and found time for public affairs becoming sheriff of his county and a member of the State Legislature. In 1857 he bought land in the Sonoma Valley forming the Buena Vista estate, some of which already produced wine — 'there were two bath houses . . . brandy distillery and a press house.' In 1857 Haraszthy himself produced 6,500 gallons of wine there. In seven years Buena Vista had over 400 acres of vineyards with wine cellars he had tunnelled into the hillside. These collapsed in the San Francisco earthquake of 1906 but have since been restored. Today in spite of a series of disasters Buena Vista has 620 acres of flourishing vineyards and is renowned for its premium wines. Haraszthy would have been astonished by its stainless-steel tanks and ultra-modern equipment but proud indeed that one of its cellars houses the headquarters of the Brotherhood of the Knights of the American Vine.

Previous page: The Napa Valley harvest of 1982.

Father Juan Ugarte, 17th-century wine pioneer.

Right: Kenwood Vineyard, Sonoma County, California.

The stone building, dating from 1864, of Buena Vista, California's oldest winery. Note the arms of Count Haraszthy, its colorful founder.

46

Neatly staked-out vineyards in Livermore Valley (above) and Napa Valley (right).

Haraszthy's contribution to California as a wine state far exceeded the success of Buena Vista and its wines. He was instrumental in getting an official commission appointed to advance viticulture in the state which he suggested should found an agricultural college, and was sent to Europe on a tour of vineyards which brought some 200,000 European vines into the state. In fact the State University of California has had its Department of Viticulture and Enology at Davis for many years now. Haraszthy disappeared mysteriously in 1869 – it was rumored that he was eaten by an alligator in Nicaragua. There can be little argument that no other single person had so profound an influence on California's wine industry.

An acquaintance and neighbor of his, a German named Charles Krug (who had no connection with the famous French champagne firm) made his first wine with a small cider press in the Napa Valley in 1858 and three years later owned his own vineyard and winery there. The winery and name still exist although the concern is now operated by the Mondavi family. In the 1870s California, in common with the rest of the United States, suffered from an economic depression which hit the wine industry and this was accompanied by the scourge of phylloxera which by the 1880s had devastated many of the vineyards. California then followed the example of Europe devastated many of the vineyards. California then followed the example of Europe by grafting on Eastern root stocks. The industry began to recover but, alas, Prohibition brought another serious setback. However, as happened elsewhere in the United States not all was lost. With repeal and the years that followed old vineyards have been able to make a new start, employing new methods and above all taking advantage of new scientific discoveries to which the now world-renowned Department of Viticulture and Enology at Davis has contributed greatly.

Today California's 300 or more vineyards and wineries produce well over 400,000,000 gallons of wine in a year. Much of it is mass produced and so, inevitably, very much *vin ordinaire*, but as the successes in international wine competitions show, a great deal of it is very good and sometimes very good indeed, particularly the dry white table wines which have now become more sought after in North America.

The most widely known wine-producing areas are, of course, the Sonoma and Napa Valleys. The Russian River (named after the Russian fur-trading post of the 19th century) which flows through the former almost parallel with the Pacific coast north of San Francisco, passes near such well-known wineries as Korbels, the Italian Swiss Colony, Cresta Blanca, Parducci etc. The Napa Valley further to the east and

An anti-frost propeller in the Napa Valley.

north can list Beaulieu, Inglenook, Louis M Martini, Beringer, Charles Krug, the Christian Brothers and many others. South of San Francisco and between that city and Los Angeles is the San Joaquin or Central Valley and here and south of it we note such distinguished names as United Vintners, E and J Gallo, the Monterey Vineyard, Paul Masson and Wente Brothers. More details of these and other Californian wineries are given in the pages that follow and go to make up a fascinating picture of determination, imagination, business acumen and sometimes romance that is typically American. Some wineries have been taken over by huge business concerns, many have remained in family hands. It should not be forgotten, too, that the state, so fortunate in its climate, is not only by far the leading wine producer in the United States, but is the biggest producer of grapes. These are not only used for making wine, but for the table as well as for making non-alcoholic drinks and brandies.

The wine-growing areas of the state have been divided by the University Department of Viticulture and Enology into five zones on the basis of the temperatures during the grape-growing period each year. The basis of the calculations was temperatures registered over 50°F from April to October in five-day periods. Thus if the average daily temperature over one such period was 65°F the calculation would be $65 - 50 = 15 \times 5 = 75$ degree days. California, fortunate though it is in sunshine, is a state of varied features with a warm sea coast, mountains and valleys and so the degree-day calculations by no means relate strictly to degrees of latitude as might be expected. Thus as will be seen from the map the hottest region, ie that with more than 4,000 degree days is found not only in the south of the state behind Los Angeles but much further north inland behind the Napa and Sonoma Valleys which themselves fall in Regions 2 and 3 with 2,500 to 3,000 degree days and 3,000 to 3,500 respectively. These two valleys produce wines similar to those, respectively, of Bordeaux and the Rhône Valley in France, but in the same latitude, further back from the coast, Region 5 produces wines more similar to those of North Africa. If climatic conditions were constant, and those of California are remarkably so, the life of the winemaker would be a good deal easier but each year can be different as was certainly the case in California in 1981. Early summer proved to be extraordinarily hot and this, combined with a preceding mild winter, resulted in a very early season with, for example, Cabernet Sauvignon grapes, usually picked in October or early November, being harvested at the end of July.

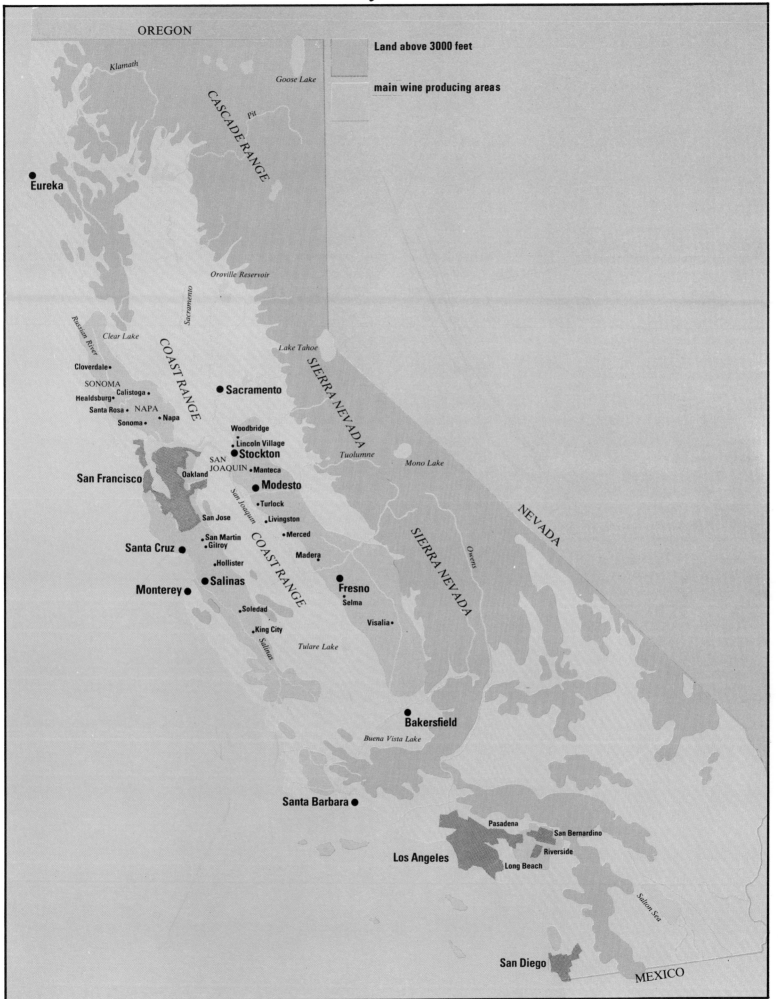

OREGON

*Klamath*

CASCADE RANGE

*Goose Lake*

*Pit*

Land above 3000 feet

main wine producing areas

● **Eureka**

*Oroville Reservoir*

*Sacramento*

*Russian River*

*Clear Lake*

COAST RANGE

*Lake Tahoe*

Cloverdale ●

SONOMA

SIERRA NEVADA

Calistoga ●

Healdsburg ●

● **Sacramento**

Santa Rosa ● NAPA

Sonoma ● ● Napa

Woodbridge

● Lincoln Village

*Tuolumne*

*Mono Lake*

SAN JOAQUIN

● **Stockton**

● Manteca

**San Francisco**

Oakland

● **Modesto**

NEVADA

*San Joaquin*

● Turlock

San Jose

● Livingston

● Merced

SIERRA NEVADA

● San Martin

● Gilroy

Madera

**Santa Cruz** ●

● Hollister

*Owens*

COAST RANGE

● **Salinas**

● **Fresno**

**Monterey** ●

● Selma

● Soledad

Visalia ●

● King City

*Salinas*

*Tulare Lake*

● **Bakersfield**

*Buena Vista Lake*

**Santa Barbara** ●

Pasadena

San Bernardino

Riverside

**Los Angeles**

Long Beach

*Salton Sea*

**San Diego**

MEXICO

NORTHERN CALIFORNIA

**Beaulieu Vineyard,** Napa Valley, Ca.
Georges de la Tour founded this winery at the end of the last century and although it is now owned (since 1969) by the Heublein Corporation the founder's name still appears on the label of their distinguished Cabernet Sauvignon Private Reserve. Most of the wines are estate bottled and include a Pinot Noir, Beauclair Johannisberg Riesling, Beaurose, Château Beaulieu (Sauvignon Blanc) and Pinot Chardonnay.

**Beringer Vineyards,** 2000 Main Street (Box 111), St Helena, Ca.
One of the famous wine names in California, Beringer's was a family concern from 1876 until the later 1960s. It was in 1876 that the young German Jacob Beringer, who had been cellarmaster at Charles Krug, acquired 97 acres just north of St Helena and built a winery. The concern flourished and enjoyed a reputation for fine wines but suffered under Prohibition although it had a license to make medicinal and sacramental wines. In 1970 it was acquired by the firm of Nestlé and Myron Nightingale, formerly assistant winemaker to Cresta Blanco Winery, became its winemaker. Its vineyards extend for nearly 2,000 acres, most of them off a 36-mile stretch of road between Napa and Knights Valley. Some still have grapes planted by the Beringer family, others as late as 1975, all with premium varietals. Since the concern was taken over, modern equipment has been installed although the original winery is still used for barrel aging, the thick rock of the tunnels dug by the Beringers providing excellent conditions. Among the new equipment are specially designed steel fermenters and special aging tanks, some of stainless steel, some of oak, from 50 gallon barrels to 12,000 gallon upright oak tanks. The capability of handling a wide variety of wines is ensured by a series of 38 1,100 gallon stainless-steel tanks as well as a series of temperature-controlled stainless-steel tanks up to 10,000 gallons in capacity. All this is reflected in the wide range of wines produced including Cabernet Sauvignon, Dry French Colombard, Chardonnay, Gewürztraminer, Gamay Beaujolais, Cabernet Sauvignon Port, Chenin Blanc and Malvasia Bianca, a 19 percent alcoholic content sweet dessert wine from grapes of that name.

The Rhine House at Beringer Vineyards.

Right: Oval-shaped German casks, 35–40 years old, used for the aging of red wines. The aging tunnels at Beringer Vineyards are over a century old. The temperature remains between 55° and 60° all year round.

Bottom right: Winemaster Myron Nightingale supervises the stacking of small French oak barrels used for the fermentation of 'Reserve' wines.

Beringer
*Napa Valley*
Gamay Beaujolais
PRODUCED AND BOTTLED BY
BERINGER VINEYARDS, ST. HELENA,

Beringer
*California*
MALVASIA BIANCA
A dessert wine, naturally fruity
and sweet, made from the Malvasia Bianca grape.
Cellared and bottled by Beringer Vineyards, St. Helena,
Napa Valley, Calif. / Alc. 19% by Vol.

Beringer
*Napa Valley*
Chenin Blanc
PRODUCED AND BOTTLED BY
BERINGER VINEYARDS, ST. HELENA, NAPA VALLEY, CALIFORNIA
ALCOHOL 12.5% BY VOLUME

The entrance to the Haraszthy Cellars of Buena Vista Vineyards, restored in 1943.

**Buena Vista Winery and Vineyards,** PO Box 182, Carneros, Sonoma. Ca.

The oldest winery in California, on the borders between the Sonoma and Napa Valleys, Buena Vista made its name in the 1860s when Count Haraszthy created its vineyards and his wines made it famous. After his death it suffered a series of setbacks, was badly affected by phylloxera and was struck by the San Francisco earthquake in 1906. In 1943 when it was bought by a newspaper executive, Frank Bartholomew, the vineyards which now extend to over 620 acres were replanted and the buildings restored and in 1971 the vineyards were again replanted this time with six grape varieties – Cabernet Sauvignon, Chardonnay, Pinot Noir, Gamay Beaujolais, Johannisberg Riesling and Gewürztraminer. The winery under the direction of Technical Director Rene Lacasia and winemaker Don Harrison has a storage capacity of 900,000 gallons and can crush 150 tons of grapes a day. Its main building, of stone, is the Haraszthy building of 1864 and the dessert wines are aged in storage tunnels dug into the hillside behind it. Buena Vista is particularly proud of its special selection bottlings – in whites Carneros Spiceling, a Gewürztraminer, a Johannisberg Riesling and a Chardonnay; in reds there is a Zinfandel, a Pinot Noir Cask 22 and a Cabernet Sauvignon. The winery, now owned by Young's

54

Markets of Los Angeles, also produces a Chablis, Gamay Blanc, Green Hungarian, Fumé Blanc in whites and a Burgundy, Gamay Beaujolais, Carneros Gamay, Pinot Noir and Cabernet Sauvignon in reds. It also makes an Ultra Dry Sherry and a Golden Cream Sherry. It is appropriate that this the oldest Californian winery should have become the national headquarters of the country's most prestigious wine society, the Brotherhood of the Knights of the American Vine, which was established in 1971 in Sacramento. Mention should also be made of the cultural activities centered at the winery including an annual series of Mozart concerts.

**Burgess Cellars,** Napa Valley, Ca.
This small winery does not grow its own grapes but buys from selected growers making among other wines Johannisberg Riesling and Cabernet Sauvignon.

**Bynum Winery,** Sonoma Valley, Ca.
A small family winery established in 1965 by a former journalist Davis Bynum. Produces among other varietal wines Chardonnay and Pinot Noir.

**Cambiasso Winery and Vineyards,** Sonoma Valley, Ca.
Founded at the end of Prohibition by an Italian family but now owned by Far Eastern interests, the winery produces Petite Sirah and Cabernet Sauvignon from its own vineyards and other wines from grapes from selected growers.

**Chappellett Vineyard,** St Helena, Napa Valley, Ca.
This small winery with a capacity of under 50,000 gallons a year produces in reds Cabernet Sauvignon and Merlot and in whites Chardonnay, Chenin Blanc and Johannisberg Riesling.

**Château Montelena,** 1429 Tubbs Lane, Calistoga, Napa Valley, Ca.
Apart from its products this winery has two claims to distinction. It is housed in what looks like a château and at its foot is a genuine Chinese garden complete with arched bridges, weeping willows and red-lacquered pavilions. The château was built in 1882 by the founder of the winery, Alfred L Tubbs, a California State Senator and owner of a whaling fleet. It has stone walls, in places 12-feet thick, running into the hillside and is in a beautiful setting at the foot of St Helena Mountain with the Napa River forming one of the vineyard's boundaries. Jade Lake in the Chinese garden was created in the 1950s by the then owners, a Chinese couple who longed

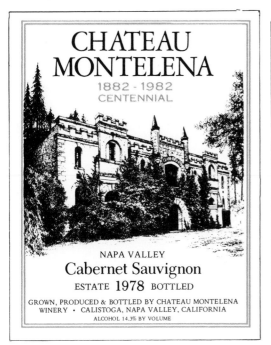

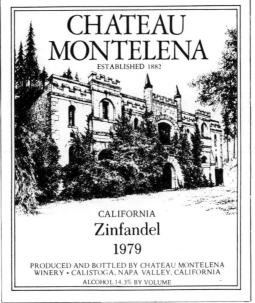

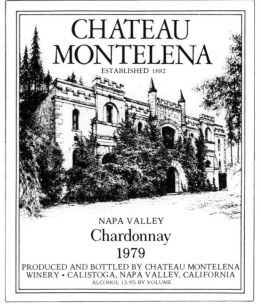

nostalgically for gardens like those of their ancestral home in China. The present owners James L Barrett, Lee J Paschich and Ernest W Hahn took over in 1972. Under its winemaker Bob Hattaway and vineyard manager John Rolleri it produces a Johannisberg Riesling, a Chardonnay, a Zinfandel and a Cabernet Sauvignon aged, as is the Chardonnay, in French oak barrels and later in the bottle. In 1976 the 1973 Chardonnay was entered in a blind tasting by eminent French experts in Paris and gained first place over nine other leading French white burgundies and California Chardonnays.

**Château St Jean Vineyards and Winery,** 8555 Sonoma Highway, Kenwood, Ca 95452.

By California standards this is a very new winery– it was founded on the estate only in 1973 – but it has already achieved a high reputation for its wines which rate as some of the best in California, which is saying quite a lot in these days. Its founders, Robert and Ed Merzoian and their brother-in-law Ken Sheffield, established dealers in California table wine grapes, would be the first to pay tribute to their winemaker, Dick Arrowood and to their Director of Vineyard Operations, Bernard Fernandez. The policy of the winery has been to confine its products to fine white varietals notably Chardonnay, Sauvignon Blanc, Gewürztraminer and Johannisberg Riesling although a small quantity of red Cabernet Sauvignon is made. It also makes, at its Graton winery, Champagne from the traditional Chardonnay and Pinot Noir grapes by the *méthode Champenoise*. Although otherwise the policy is to limit production to the four white varietals mentioned this does not mean that only four wines are produced. The policy is one of vineyard appellation, that is to say wines are identified by the vineyards in which the grapes were grown. Thus in 1980 10 separate Chardonnays were made. Some of the vineyards belong to Château St Jean which has 105 acres under cultivation, and at least 30 percent of the winery's requirements will continue to be grown on these, but for the rest Château St Jean purchases from selected growers, mostly in Sonoma County, with whom personal relations and commitments have developed. The Château's own wines include Chardonnay, Pinot Blanc, Gewürztraminer, Johannisberg Riesling, Muscat Canelli and Sauvignon Blanc. The winery does not plan to expand vastly, aiming at something between 50,000 and 80,000 gallons annually and its modern equipment has been installed with this and the vineyard appellation policy in mind. Apart from its 1,200 55-gallon capacity oak storage barrels it has a large number of very small stainless-steel, temperature-controlled fermentation tanks, some under 500-gallon capacity, none over 3,500 gallons. Among the vineyard appellations already becoming well known are Robert Young, Belle Terre, Redwood Valley, Wildwood and Forrest Crimmins Ranch. A word must also be said about the handsome and picturesque building, more like a château than most American wineries with that name, which stands backed by the Sugarloaf Ridge, the country described by Jack London in *The Valley of the Moon* where his hero found happiness.

Brother Timothy and a fellow priest sample the wares of the Christian Brothers' vineyards, at Mont La Salle, Napa.

The picturesque Château St Jean winery.

56

Brother Timothy checks the huge storage vats in Greystones on the northern outskirts of St Helena.

**The Christian Brothers,** Mont la Salle, nr St Helena, Napa Valley, Ca.
The Brothers are a lay religious teaching order of the Roman Catholic Church and their training school was established at Martinez near San Francisco in 1879. There were already 12 acres of vineyards on the property and the Brothers soon turned to winemaking for their own and sacramental purposes and commercial wine production had by 1887 become a sideline to their educational and religious work. Today

the Brothers have 150 acres of vineyards at Mont la Salle in the foothills of the Napa Valley, 1,250 acres in the Napa Valley near St Helena, and 200 acres in the San Joaquin Valley to the south where it has wineries at Fresno and Reedley. 'Greystones,' the imposing stone winery on the northern outskirts of St Helena was bought by the Brothers in 1950 and was visited by no fewer than 361,000 people in 1981. Here the Brothers make their Champagnes and age their premium wines in oak casks and barrels and in redwood tanks. Not all the grapes used are grown on the Brothers' vineyards, extensive though they are — their cellars have a total storage and aging capacity of 9,500,000 gallons — and they buy from selected growers who grow to

The Mont La Salle vineyard of the Christian Brothers.

their particular specifications and needs. The winemaking operations are directed by Brothers David and Timothy, the latter the cellarmaster, who manages and supervises all the winemaking activities of their lay staff from growing the grapes to aging, blending and bottling. Their wines include Cabernet Sauvignon, Gewürztraminer, Champagne Brut and Extra Dry, an estate-bottled Pineau de la Loire, Chardonnay, Zinfandel, Pinot St Georges, Napa Fumé and a light sweet wine from Muscat grapes, Château la Salle. Dessert wines and brandy are made at Reedley. Although the Brothers' wine operations are run on commercial lines, the profits after tax deductions go to help pay for their teaching and religious activities.

**Clos du Val Wine Co Ltd,** 5330 Silverado Trail, Napa, Ca.

Small and comparatively new — it was started in 1972 — this winery lies about eight miles north of Napa. Its winemaker is a Frenchman, Bernard Portet, and the vineyards extend for 120 acres. They are planted with Cabernet Sauvignon, Merlot and Zinfandel grapes. The Cabernet is made according to the Médoc tradition with a blend of Cabernet Sauvignon and Merlot. The Zinfandel, with a high alcoholic content of 15 percent, is made of 100 percent Zinfandel grapes grown on two different soils. One, rocky, it is claimed gives powerful body and deep color. The other, gravelly to loamy, gives freshness and fruitiness. Bernard Portet, who matures the wines in small French oak barrels, claims to combine the best traditional methods of the French Médoc region with the use of modern American technology. The varietals produced by Clos du Val are Cabernet Sauvignon, Merlot, Zinfandel and Chardonnay.

**Concannon Vineyard,** 4590 Tesla Road, Livermore, Ca.

This 300-acre vineyard in the Livermore Valley, 30 miles east of San Francisco, has been in existence since 1883 when James Concannon, a 36-year-old Irish-born American, planted it to produce wine for sacramental purposes. He was no mean judge. He chose the Livermore Valley because soil and climate seemed very similar to those of the Bordeaux area of France and very soon he was also producing wines for the table. Today it is his grandson who is President of the company. Wines produced today include a red varietal Petite Sirah, Sauvignon Blanc, Muscat Blanc, California Chablis, Livermore Riesling and a Chardonnay whose grapes come from vineyards in three different counties.

The entrance to Concannon Vineyards at Livermore.

Left: Cabernet grapes ripen in the vineyards of the Clos du Val Wine Co.

Below: Oak barrels copied from the French Médoc region mature the Clos du Val vintage.

**Domaine Chandon,** Napa Valley, Ca.
Champagne drinkers will recognize this famous name and the winery was indeed founded by the famous Rheims firm of Moet and Chandon. This was in 1973 and the Domaine already produces noteworthy Chandon Napa Valley Brut and Blanc de Noir.

**Dry Creek Vineyards,** Sonoma Valley, Ca.
These extend for 50 acres and were planted in 1972. The winery produces Cabernet Sauvignon, Gamay and Zinfandel in reds, and Chardonnay, Chenin Blanc and a Fumé Blanc in whites.

The potential of the S...
to make exceptional ...
secret kept by a small ...
nia winemakers and ...
year in Mendocino C...
of Sauvignon Blanc ar...
Sauvignon Blanc gra...
vines gain greater va...
distinction.

Our 1981 fume' Blanc...
Blanc. the grapes we...
proximately 22.3° B...
mented at slightly w...
than past vintages, at ...
was aged in American ...
rels for two months.

**fetzer**

1981
mendocino

**fume'blanc**
dry sauvignon blanc

produced and bottled by fetzer vineyards
redwood valley, california, u.s.a. alcohol 12.3% by volume

*John E.*

fetzer vineyar...

---

1980
ricetti zinfandel

On a sloped mountain hillside of red clay soil, the Ricetti vineyard of Redwood Valley receives an ideal northern exposure. The 22-year-old vines are devoted entirely to Zinfandel grapes. These grapes have consistently produced Zinfandel wines of pronounced flavor and strong varietal character. 1980 is the 12th year we have made a special Zinfandel from the Ricetti vineyard.

In 1980, the Ricetti Zinfandel was harvested at 26° Brix on October 11, fermented warm and pressed before completely dry, it rested in small American oak barrels from April 1981 until February 1982. the wine was fined with fresh egg whites and lightly filtered before bottling.

**fetzer**

1980
ricetti
mendocino
**zinfandel**

produced and bottled by fetzer vineyards
redwood valley, california, u.s.a. alcohol 15.7% by volume

*John E. Fetzer*

fetzer vineyards

---

**Fetzer Vineyards,** PO Box 227, Redwood Valley, Ca.

Mention has been made of family-run wineries but Fetzer Vineyards really does deserve the title for Bernard Fetzer and his wife Kathleen who started the business in 1958 have 11 children and nine of them, brothers and sisters, work in the winery and have done so since childhood. Redwood Valley is in Mendocino County which borders on the Pacific north of San Francisco. The original 70-acre vineyard bought by Bernard Fetzer has expanded to 200 acres and Sundial Ranch with another 200 acres of vines at Hopland, 20 miles to the south, was acquired in 1981. These provide 20 percent of their requirements, the remainder is bought from other neighboring vineyards but not blended. In other words each vineyard wine is made separately. Red wines are aged in American oak barrels and dry whites in French Limousin oak barrels. There are two separate wineries, one for making red wines, one for the white. The red wines are: Cabernet Sauvignon, Ricetti Zinfandel, Pinot Noir, Gamay Beaujolais and Petite Sirah. The whites: Chardonnay, Fumé Blanc, French Colombard (described as 'highly fruity wine of appley-spice crispness,') Chenin Blanc, Johannisberg Riesling and Gewürztraminer. The Ricetti Zinfandel, from grapes from the Ricetti vineyard, deserves special mention for its alcoholic content is no less than 15.7 percent by volume. The winery is to be congratulated on the unusually full descriptions on its labels.

**Foppiano Wine Company,** Healsburg, Sonoma, Ca.

A family concern which has turned from bulk production to varietals on its 200 acres. Produces Cabernet Sauvignon, Petite Sirah and Pinot Noir.

**Freemark Abbey Winery,** PO Box 410, 3022 St Helena Highway North, St Helena, Ca.

This winery has at least one claim to fame – it was the first winery in California to be built by a woman which, in 1886, was quite a feat. Phylloxera forced her to sell eight years later. Another claim to fame was that it was once owned by a San Francisco hotelier whose surname was Swig. In 1965 it was purchased by the present owners who acquired the 148-acre Red Barn Branch and have planted 130 acres of it with grapes. In 1973 the winery was extended to provide storage space, bottling room, laboratory etc and it now has a production capacity of 24,000 cases per year. Despite their comparative youth Freemark Abbey Wines have achieved a good reputation and include: Johannisberg Riesling, Chardonnay, Cabernet Sauvignon and Cabernet Bosché, and Edelwein from botrytized ('noble rot') grapes.

**Guenoc Winery,** PO Box 1146, 21000 Bulls Canyon Road, Middletown, Ca.

Not much can be said at this stage about this winery because, started in the early 1970s, it has only just come into production. There is however a great deal to be said about its history. Few people know that the famous British actress Lily Langtry, the 'Jersey Lily,' mistress of King Edward VII, actually planted vineyards and

FREEMARK ABBEY

1978
NAPA VALLEY
**CABERNET BOSCHÉ**
*(Cabernet Sauvignon)*

PRODUCED AND BOTTLED BY
FREEMARK ABBEY WINERY, ST. HELENA, CALIFORNIA, USA
Alcohol 13.0% by volume

Above: The bottling line at Freemark Abbey.

Right: Fining wine at Freemark Abbey.

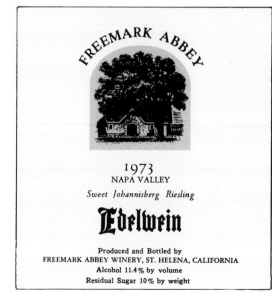

FREEMARK ABBEY

1973
NAPA VALLEY

*Sweet Johannisberg Riesling*

**Edelwein**

Produced and Bottled by
FREEMARK ABBEY WINERY, ST. HELENA, CALIFORNIA
Alcohol 11.4% by volume
Residual Sugar 10% by weight

imported a winemaker from Bordeaux, France to make her wines. Even fewer know that she did so at her home in Guenoc Valley in California's Lake County. What happened is not recorded but in the 1960s Orville Magoon, an engineer, and his brother, Eaton (with theatrical connections in London, England) and the Magoon family acquired a 23,000-acre ranch in the valley, including Lily's house. They set out to revive the vineyard and winery and their first wines were released in the fall of 1982.

Below: Heitz Wine Cellars.

**Heitz Wine Cellars,** 436 St Helena Highway, Sonoma, Ca.

Heitz Wine Cellars is by no means one of the oldest wineries of the Napa Valley but it is certainly among the most prestigious. Its Martha's Vineyard Cabernet Sauvignon is one of the most highly thought of California wines (the 1974 vintage retails at $60 per bottle). The present winery was started in 1961 by Joe Heitz, who is President of what is a family concern. During World War II he had been a ground crewman in a fighter squadron in California and supplemented his service pay by working as a cellarman in a winery. He became interested in wine and when the war ended studied enology at the University of California in Davis and after graduating worked as a winemaker and taught winemaking at Fresno State College. In the early 1960s he and his wife Alice started their winery in Spring Valley just east of St Helena, an old established vineyard and winery begun in 1880. They use grapes not only from their own vineyards but selected growths from other growers. The renowned Martha's Vineyard is named after one of these, the vineyard of Tom

1980
NĀPĀ VĀLLEY
**CHARDONNAY**
ALCOHOL 13% BY VOLUME
PRODUCED AND BOTTLED IN OUR CELLAR BY
**HEITZ WINE CELLĀRS**
ST. HELENA, CALIFORNIA

1979
NĀPĀ VĀLLEY
**GRIGNOLINO**
ALCOHOL 13% BY VOLUME
PRODUCED AND BOTTLED IN OUR CELLAR BY
**HEITZ WINE CELLĀRS**
ST. HELENA, CALIFORNIA

| VINTAGE 1977 | BOTTLED JULY, 1981 |
|---|---|
| Bottle | of a total of 32,400 Bottles |
| Magnum | of a total of, 600 Magnums |

NĀPĀ VĀLLEY
**CĀBERNET SĀUVIGNON**
ALCOHOL 13½% BY VOLUME
PRODUCED AND BOTTLED IN OUR CELLAR BY
**HEITZ WINE CELLĀRS**
ST. HELENA, CALIFORNIA

MARTHA'S VINEYARD

and Martha May at Oakville, and is the special responsibility of Joe's eldest son David, another Davis graduate, who is also responsible for the winery's Johannisberg Riesling. The winery's red wines are fermented first in stainless-steel containers and then in oak tanks or barrels. Its products also include Cabernet Sauvignon from the Bella Oaks vineyard, Pinot Noir, Grignolino Rosé, Chablis, Gewürztraminer, Brut and Extra Dry Champagne and a 'Cellar Treasure' sherry and port.

**Inglenook Vineyard**, Rutherford, Napa, Ca.
A large winery with a long history which, like Beaulieu Vineyard, is now owned by the Heublein Corporation. It produces distinguished wines including Cabernet Sauvignon, Gamay, Pinot Noir, Chenin Blanc, Traminer and White Pinot.

**Italian Swiss Colony**, Asti, Sonoma, Ca.
Another winery owned by the Heublein Corporation, this is one of the giants of the California wine industry capable of producing 8,000,000 gallons. It was founded in 1881 by an Italian immigrant Andrea Sbarbaro who died in 1923 when it was taken over by a giant member-growers' cooperative which later gave way to Heublein. It makes some premium wines under a Private Stock label but the emphasis is on drinkable but not highly distinguished wines at medium prices.

**F Korbel & Brothers**, Sonoma, Ca.
One of the earliest names in California wine history (it was founded in 1860) this winery is known for its California Champagne made by the *méthode Champenoise* – Korbel Sec, Extra Dry, Brut and Natural – and other sparkling wines.

**Hanns Kornell Champagne Cellars**, Larkmead Lane, St Helena, Ca 94574.
As its name indicates this winery, in the Napa Valley, is devoted entirely to the production of Champagne. It is done by the *méthode Champenoise*, that is, it is fermented entirely in the bottle. The winery's history is very much an American story. The founder, Hanns Kornell fled in 1940 from Nazi Germany, arriving penniless in the United States. For several generations the family had produced wine in Germany and Hanns was no exception. It took him 12 years, washing dishes and doing other jobs and later as Champagne master for other wineries before he could rent his own winery in Sonoma. Even then he had to make his living by selling wine from an old truck until his own wines were ready. In 1958 he bought the old Larkmead Cellars in the nearby Napa Valley and since then with the help of his

American wife, Marilouise, son and daughter, he has concentrated on fine Champagnes which have been highly successful not only in the United States but abroad. His Sehr Trocken, a Champagne made mainly from Riesling grapes won a gold medal in London, England in 1981, the Brut a similar award in 1980 as well as in Milan, Italy that same year. The Extra Dry, from Sémillon, Sauvignon Blanc and Chenin Blanc grapes won a Diploma of Honor with Gold Medal in Yugoslavia in 1980 and 1981 and silver medals in London in the same years. Other wines are Rouge, a red Champagne from Pinot Noir Grapes, and Muscat Alexandria.

**Charles Krug Winery,** PO Box 191, St Helena, Ca.
Charles Krug is one of the leading names in California wine history but, although the winery retains the name, it is now owned by C Mondavi and Sons. The original Charles Krug was born in Prussia in 1825 and was 27 when he arrived in San Francisco. He became a pioneer in 1858 when he made the first wine made in Napa Valley by then modern methods, using a small cider press. By 1861 he had his own vineyards and winery near that of his acquaintance, Count Haraszthy, and soon his wine had achieved a high reputation which it maintains today under Mondavi and Sons. They use the Krug winery building, pictured on their label, rebuilt in 1874 (the original 1861 building was destroyed by fire) which is set among fine oaks and surrounded by well-kept vineyards. They produce a Napa Valley Cabernet Sauvignon, Merlot, Zinfandel, Chardonnay, Gewürztraminer, Chenin Blanc, Johannisberg Riesling and Grey Riesling and a California Vin Rosé.

**Louis M Martini,** St Helena, Ca.
This winery produces some of the best-known wines in North America. Its annual production amounts to some 800,000 gallons from the 900 acres of its five separate vineyards in the Sonoma as well as the Napa Valley. It is very much a family concern and was founded in 1922 as Louis M Martini Grape Products Co by Louis Michael Martini, an Italian immigrant. As a boy he helped his father supply fish to the restaurants and markets of San Francisco and as a sideline his father developed a small business distributing table wines. When he was 18 Louis was sent to Genoa for an intensive course in enology at the university there and on his return worked in vineyards to get practical experience. It was in 1936, three years after the repeal

Below: The Martini family.
Right: top to bottom, the entrance to the winery at St Helena; the aging cellar, oak casks and bins for wood and bottle aging of Vintage Varietal wines; and a view of one of their Sonoma vineyards.

66

of Prohibition, that he bought the 575-acre Monte Rosso vineyard in the Sonoma Valley. It had been planted in the 1880s. In the next 36 years the winery was to acquire four more vineyards, three in the Napa Valley — La Loma (240 acres), Las Amigas (140 acres) and Glen Oak (980 acres) — and one more in the Sonoma Valley, Los Vinedos del Rio (172 acres). Their soil varies from red decomposed volcanic rock to clay loam and their elevation from 40 to 1,200 feet. Not surprisingly they yield a wide variety of grapes — Cabernet Sauvignon, Pinot Noir, Merlot, Barbera, Zinfandel, Gamay Beaujolais, Chardonnay, Johannisberg Riesling, Gewürztraminer, Folle Blanche, dry Chenin Blanc. These varietals are of high quality and highly regarded as premium table wines. The winery also produces Pale Dry Sherry, Cream Sherry and Muscat Amabile.

**Mayacamas Vineyards,** Napa Valley, Ca.
These stand 2,000 feet above sea level on the mountain range separating the Napa and Sonoma Valleys. Wines produced include Chardonnay, Chenin Blanc, Zinfandel Rosé and a sweet wine from botrytized Sauvignon and Sémillon grapes.

**Robert Mondavi Winery,** Oakville, Napa Valley, Ca.
The famous Charles Krug Winery (p 66) is now owned and run by the Mondavi family except for Robert Mondavi who used to work with them but left in 1966. He then bought this property in the San Joaquin Valley and started what is one of California's most prestigious wineries. He is now aided by his two sons Tim and Michael. Michael who is President of the company looks after marketing and planning while Tim, a graduate of the University of California, Davis is the wine-

Harvesting the grapes at Robert Mondavi's To-Kalon Vineyard in the Napa Valley.

maker. Robert, now in his 60s, is anything but a spent force and plays a considerable part in the whole operation. After all it was he who in 1979 entered into an alliance with no less a person than Baron Philippe de Rothschild to produce a California equivalent of the Baron's renowned Château Mouton-Rothschild. The Robert Mondavi Winery's vineyard, alongside the striking winery built to Robert's order in 1966, extends for some 700 acres and may well reach 1,000 or thereabouts soon. They also have another vineyard in the valley. The winery produces a Reserve Cabernet Sauvignon of exceptional quality, and a Sauvignon Blanc (Fumé Blanc), of both of which it is very proud, Petite Sirah, Chardonnay and Pinot Noir.

**McDowell Valley Vineyard,** 3811 Highway 175, McDowell Valley,
Mendocino County, Hopland, Ca.
In January 1982 McDowell Valley was officially designated by Washington as a viticultural area. Two years earlier Richard and Karen Keehn had bought 360 acres of what had already been vineyard land and began a varietal improvement program followed in 1979 by the building of California's first comprehensive solar-integrated winery. The winemaking is in the capable hands of winemaker George Bursick, a Master of Enology from the State University, Davis. The vineyards contain seven different types of soil and have been planted with 12 different varieties of grapes. The winery already produces Chenin Blanc, Fumé Blanc (from Sauvignon Blanc grapes), Chardonnay, Grenache (rosé), Cabernet Sauvignon, Zinfandel and Petite Sirah.

**Parducci Wine Cellars,** 501 Parducci Road, Ukiah, Mendocino County, Ca.
One of the more northerly of the California wineries it was founded by Adolph

The Parducci winery standing in its vineyard in the north of California.

The slopes of Joseph Phelps' vineyard with the Napa Valley in the background.

Experts check on the Parducci vines. . . .

Parducci in 1931. Anticipating the repeal of Prohibition by two years he planted his 'Home Ranch' vineyard, which surrounds the winery, mainly with French Colombard and Petite Sirah. Later the Talmadge Vineyard, five miles to the south, was planted with Chenin Blanc, Cabernet Sauvignon, Pinot Noir and Gamay Beaujolais and in 1971 the Largo Vineyard was planted with Chardonnay, Sauvignon Blanc and Chenin Blanc. Apart from wines with these names Parduccis make a Zinfandel, a Maywine, a light white flavored with woodruff herbs and strawberry concentrate, and a sweet white table wine Flora, made from grapes of that name. The winemaker is John Parducci, son of the founder.

**Joseph Phelps,** St Helena, Ca.
Joseph Phelps, who gave the winery its name and is its owner, used to be a construction engineer. He now runs some food shops and the winery on which, since he acquired it in 1973, he has lavished loving attention. In this he is aided by one of California's best-known and most respected winemakers, Walter Schug. The winery stands on a 670-acre estate, formerly a cattle ranch, on the east side of the Napa Valley. Nearly 200 of the 670 acres are planted with vines and to the original estate have been added another 70 acres on cooler land, but further additions are contemplated. Phelps and Schug are both imaginative and courageous in their experimentation and the high reputation their wines have achieved in less than a decade of growth pays tribute to this. The achievement – planting began only in 1974 – is indeed remarkable especially since many of their wines are aged for up to two years before being bottled. One speciality is their botrytized Late Harvest Johannisberg Riesling but they are proud of all their wines particularly Eisele and Backus, two Cabernet Sauvignons and Insignia, a much respected red. The winery produces some 50,000 cases each year and its wines include: Gewürztraminer, some botrytized, Zinfandel, Cabernet Sauvignon, Chardonnay, Sauvignon Blanc, Petite Sirah and Pinot Noir.

**Raymond Vineyard and Cellar,** 849 Zinfandel Lane, St Helena, Ca.
Another of the young California wineries, Raymonds started off only in 1970 when Roy Raymond, who was winemaker at Beringers, and his wife bought an 80-acre vineyard belonging to that concern and started in business on their own, or rather with their two sons Roy Junior and Walt. Roy Senior's wife is a granddaughter of the Jacob Beringer who founded that famous winery and the two sons had both

worked in it. Today Roy Jr manages the vineyards and Walt is the winemaker. They grow their own grapes, all cordon pruned, but also manage new vineyards for others which will add to their supply. The winery has given up, at least temporarily, production of its Pinot Noir and Zinfandel to concentrate on their estate-bottled Cabernet Sauvignon and Chardonnay as their leading wines with Johannisberg Riesling and Chenin Blanc as secondary varieties.

**Schramsberg Vineyards,** Calistoga, Ca.
This small but distinguished winery concentrates on making Champagne by the traditional *méthode Champenoise*. It has been run, since 1965, by Jack and Jamie Davies, he a former businessman, she formerly owner of an art gallery, but the winery has a much longer history. It was founded in 1862 by a German immigrant, Jacob Schram, and for long enjoyed a high reputation, but when the Davies bought it, it had closed down and was in a sorry state. Today the cellars, tunnels dug 175 feet into the hillside by Chinese laborers over a 100 years ago, are once more stacked with Champagne bottles in the tens of thousands. The vineyards which once covered 100 acres are now only 40 acres in extent and the Davies buy grapes from other vineyards, but they adhere strictly to the *méthode Champenoise* tradition, although they are experimenting with a mechanical *remuage*. Their Blanc de Noirs is made from Pinot Noir and Chardonnay, the Blanc de Blancs from Pinot Blanc and Chardonnay grapes. They also make a Cuvée de Pinot, a pink Champagne from Pinot Noir and Napa Gamay grapes, and a demisec Crémant made mainly from the Flora grape which is a cross between Riesling and Sémillon. Greg Fowler is the winemaker. The winery proudly boasts that not only have their wines been used at inaugural ceremonies in Washington DC but that on one occasion, in 1972, their

. . . and on the Schramsberg Champagne.

**Schramsberg**
FOUNDED 1862

## BLANC DE NOIRS

NAPA VALLEY
CHAMPAGNE

VINTAGE 1978

PRODUCED AND BOTTLED BY
SCHRAMSBERG VINEYARDS
CALISTOGA, CALIFORNIA

ALCOHOL 12.5% BY VOLUME
CONTENTS 750 MLS

SCHRAMSBERG    SCHRAMSBERG

The Schramsberg, high on the westerly slopes
of the Napa Valley.

Champagnes were flown to Peking for the delectation of American and Chinese party leaders during the visit of former President Richard Nixon.

**Sebastiani Vineyards,** Sonoma Valley, Ca.
Another California giant, founded by Samuele Sebastiani in 1904, it has a 5,000,000 gallon capacity, but is still run by the founder's family. It began by making wine for other bottlers but started to make its own premium wines in 1954. It makes a score of table wines from grapes bought mostly from selected growers. Noteworthy among its wines are a Cabernet Sauvignon and a particularly good Barbera.

**Sonoma Vineyards,** Windsor, Sonoma, Ca.
Another of the big wineries with a 3,000,000 gallon capacity from its 1,500 acres of vineyards.

**Spring Mountain Vineyards,** 285 Spring Mountain Road, St Helena, Ca 94574.
Television viewers are very familiar with this winery for a great deal of the CBS television series *Falcon Crest* is filmed at Spring Mountain and it is not surprising that the winery has started to use the name on its labels with Spring Mountain Falcon Crest Napa Valley Chardonnay. The winery is small and was founded in 1968 by a San Francisco business man and wine lover, Michael Robbins, who believes that winemaking is 'the last of the romantic businesses.' The winery has some 35 acres of planted vineyards surrounding it with a total of 100 to be planted soon. More grapes come from other vineyards owned by Robbins in the Napa Valley. Production has grown from some 3,000 cases annually in the early years to 25,000 cases and although the range of its wines is limited, or perhaps because of that, a high quality is maintained by winemaker John Williams. Among their wines are Cabernet Sauvignon (blended with seven percent Merlot and four percent Cabernet Franc), Sauvignon Blanc, aged in oak, 'Mariage' a Pinot Noir, 'Les Trois Cuvées' a blend of Pinot Noir, and Chardonnay.

Above: The impressive slopes of Sterling Vineyards' Diamond Mountain vineyard in the Napa Valley.

Right: Small aging casks in Sterling Vineyards' cellars.

**Stag's Leap Wine Cellars,** 5766 Silverado Trail, Napa, Ca 94558.
This is a small winery started only in 1970. Its 44 acres of vineyard are planted with 40 acres of Cabernet Sauvignon and four with Merlot. The other grapes they require – they produce some 25,000 cases of wine annually – are bought from other selected growers. Varietals produced include Cabernet Sauvignon, Merlot, Chardonnay, White Riesling and Gamay Beaujolais.

**Sterling Vineyards,** 1111 Dunaweal Lane, Calistoga, Ca.
Since 1978 this select winery in the Napa Valley has limited its production to four fine varietal wines – Cabernet Sauvignon, Merlot, Chardonnay and Sauvignon Blanc. Owned by the Coca-Cola Company, its chief winemaker is Theo Rosenbrand, originally from the Netherlands, who has been in the wine business for nearly 30 years and whose professed claim and achievement is to produce fine, elegant wines. It was for this reason that the decision to reduce the number of wines to four was reached. In the European tradition the 500 acres of vineyard at Calistoga, near St Helena in the Napa Valley, surround the winery which is built in the Moorish style with stained glass windows in its white walls, Moorish fountains etc. A feature of a visit is the aerial tramway trip from the winery to the 500-feet high vineyard.

The Sauvignon Blanc wine made from the grapes of that name blended with Sémillon is aged in barrels of French oak and later for two to three years in the bottle. The Merlot, with a 13 percent alcohol content, compares favorably with French wines from Pomerol and St Emilion in Bordeaux and the Reserve Cabernet Sauvignon, a blend of Cabernet Sauvignon and Merlot, is the pride of the winery. Winery and vineyard being together, Sterling rightly label their wine 'estate bottled' — the equivalent of France's 'Château bottled.'

**Stonegate Winery,** 1183 Dunaweal Lane, Calistoga, Ca.
This winery is small and new but is already registering success in local wine competitions. Situated just north of St Helena in the Napa Valley its owners are James and Barbara Spaulding and the winemaker their son David. The Spauldings founded the winery in 1973. They now have 15 acres of vineyard surrounding the winery which is on the valley floor and a further 20 acres, the Spaulding Vineyard, terraced out of the steep slopes above between 800 and 1,000 feet high. Their grape supply is supplemented from the Kortum Canyon and Bella Vista Vineyards, both close neighbors of the Spaulding Vineyard. From the 15 acres round the winery come an estate-bottled Sauvignon Blanc and a French Colombard as well as a Chardonnay and a Cabernet Sauvignon. From the Spaulding Vineyard come a Chardonnay and a Merlot.

**Stony Hill Vineyard,** St Helena, Napa, Ca.
A small winery — its vineyard covers only 38 acres — it has a high reputation producing among other wines Chardonnay, Gewürztraminer, Sémillon and White Riesling.

**Sutter Home Winery Inc,** PO Box 248, St Helena, Ca.
The feature of this 100 percent family-owned business is its concentration on a one-grape variety wine in limited quantities designed to preserve quality. The grape is the Zinfandel and it is grown not in the Napa Valley where the wine is made but

**WENTE BROS.**

1978

MONTEREY

**PINOT NOIR**

PRODUCED AND BOTTLED BY WENTE BROS.
LIVERMORE, CALIFORNIA, U.S.A.
ALCOHOL 12½% BY VOLUME

**WENTE BROS.**

1979
VINTAGE

MONTEREY

**PINOT BLANC**

PRODUCED AND BOTTLED BY WENTE BROS.
LIVERMORE, CALIFORNIA, U.S.A.
ALCOHOL 12½% BY VOLUME

some 70 miles to the east in old goldmining country in Amador County, 1,700 feet up in the foothills of the Sierra Nevada. The growing season in Amador County is intensely hot and the sugar content of the grapes (about 24° Brix) rises higher than elsewhere with a resulting high alcoholic content. The outcome, according to one American wine writer, is 'the biggest, richest, spiciest, most intensely flavored red wines produced anywhere in the nation.' The winery is owned by the Trinchero family of Italian origin who bought it in the 1940s but it was not until 1969 that Louis 'Bob' Trinchero, now President and winemaker and son of one of the founders, was introduced to the Amador County grapes. This was by way of some home-made wine provided by a friend. Within a week he had bought 20 tons of the grapes and since then has bought almost the whole crop of the Deaver Ranch. The winery produces an Amador County Zinfandel, an Eldorado County Dessert Zinfandel and a California White Zinfandel. It also makes a Muscat Amabila, a light, fruity dessert wine.

**Wente Brothers,** 5565 Tesla Road, Livermore, Ca.
1883 was a historic year in Livermore Valley for it was then, while James Concannon was establishing the Concannon Vineyard, that Carl H Wente, attracted to it for the same reasons, also founded one of North America's best-known wineries. The 50-acre vineyard he planted in the valley has since been expanded to 850 acres and new vineyards of 600 acres acquired in the cooler Monterey region bring the total vineyard area to approximately 1,450 acres. The emphasis is on the production of French-origin wines. The vineyards are managed by the founder's great grandsons Eric P Wente and Philip R Wente. Eric who has a Master's degree in Food Science looks after the winemaking. Philip with a Bachelor's degree in Agricultural Science and Business Management looks after the vineyards. Between them they produce 14 different wines including: Johannisberg Riesling, Sauvignon Blanc, Dry Sémillon, Pinot Blanc, Pinot Chardonnay (with grapes from four California regions), Gamay Beaujolais, Zinfandel, Petite Sirah, Pinot Noir, Reserve White Wine (a basis of Chenin Blanc with small quantities of White Riesling and Pinot Blanc), Blanc de Blancs (a Chenin Blanc with White Riesling and Ugni Blanc grapes added).

**ZD Wines,** 8383 Silverado Trail, Napa, Ca 94558.
Started only in 1969 ZD Wines were able to boast that one of their wines, a Chardonnay 1979, appeared on menus at the White House on the occasion of the visits of the Prime Minister of Singapore and the President of the Philippines Republic in 1982. It must have meant the realization of a dream for Z and D, Z being Gino

Z and D: Z on the left, is Gino Zepponi; on the right, Norman de Leuze.

Zepponi and D, Norman de Leuze, whose winery in 1969 consisted of half a farm storage shed. In that first year they produced 350 cases. Today, since they moved into their present winery in 1979, production is around 9,000 cases annually. They do not grow their own grapes — their very small vineyard next to the winery, planted with Chardonnay grapes, is not in production yet — but they buy from selected growers in other parts of California, much from the Tepusquet Vineyard 300 miles to the south. De Leuze is the winemaker, assisted by his son Robert, but both founders of the firm are Burgundy lovers and ZD now concentrates on Pinot Noir and Chardonnay with some Cabernet Sauvignon, having abandoned Zinfandel and Riesling in 1981.

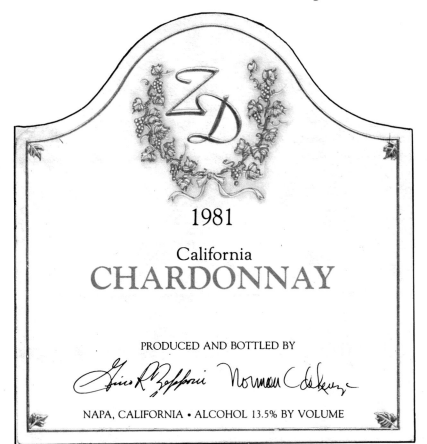

## SOUTHERN CALIFORNIA AND CENTRAL VALLEY

**Almadén Vineyards,** 153 Blossom Hill Road, San José, Ca 95118.
One of the giants of the California wine industry, and therefore, that of the United States – its Cienega Cellars figure in the Guinness Book of Records as the largest under one roof in the world – it is also one of the oldest. It was founded in 1852 by a Frenchman, Charles Lefranc, and his father-in-law Etienne Thée from Bordeaux. They acquired their first vineyard in Santa Clara County near a quick-silver mine with the Moorish name for 'the mine' Almadén. They quickly dug up the Spanish Mission grapevines which were common in California in those days, replacing them with European vines. By 1880 Lefranc had inherited his father-in-law's property and was cultivating 130 acres of vineyard with vines from Champagne, Bordeaux, Burgundy and the Rhône Valley and by 1887 was producing 100,000 gallons of wine a year. In that same year Lefranc was crushed to death trying to stop a team of stampeding horses. Today Almadén is owned by the National Distillers and Chemical Corporation and cultivates thousands of acres of vineyards. Its Distribution Center stands on a 10-acre site and has a bottle-aging capacity of almost 2,000,000 cases. It produces some 40 different varieties of wine including the distinguished 'Charles Lefranc (a founder's wine)' labeled Pinot St George, Cabernet Sauvignon, Zinfandel Royale, San Benito County Maison Blanc and Maison Rouge, Monterey County Fumé Blanc, Johannisberg Riesling, Chardonnay, Gewürztraminer. Its Champagnes are a California Brut, Chardonnay Nature (dry), Blanc de Blancs and Le Domaine, extra-dry. They also make a sparkling bronze-pink wine called Eye of the Partridge. Other wines include Pinot Noir, Sémillon, Sauvignon Blanc, Gray Riesling, Grenache Rosé, Flor Fino (dry) Sherry, Cocktail Sherry and Tinta Tawny Port. Almadén also produces Vermouth and Centennial Brandy. Its Mountain Red Wine is a popular favorite.

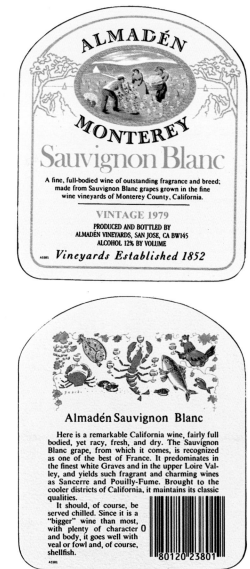

Harvest time at the Almadén Vineyards, San José.

VINTAGE 1978

## Charles Lefranc
*A Founder's Wine*

MONTEREY COUNTY
Pinot St. George

The Pinot St. George grape is not widely grown in California.
It yields a majestic red wine with an intensity of character
unmatched by any other red variety. The body is extremely
full with overwhelming richness of taste and bouquet.

PRODUCED AND BOTTLED BY
ALMADÉN VINEYARDS, SAN JOSE, CA    BW 145
ALCOHOL 12.5% BY VOLUME

SINCE 1852

## ALMADÉN
CENTENNIAL
## BRANDY

A remarkable small oak barrel-aged Brandy, Full-flavored,
its Great Finesse and Richness due solely to the Care
with which it was Distilled and the Exceptional
Conditions under which it was Matured.

EIGHTY PROOF

BLENDED AND BOTTLED BY ALMADÉN BRANDIES, ELMWOOD PL., OH.

ALMADÉN

CALIFORNIA SPARKLING WINE
## Eye of the Partridge
OEIL DE PERDRIX
CUVÉE 1981

A superb, bottle fermented, sparkling wine with great bouquet and
distinctive character. Made from grapes of the Pinot varieties, it has
the unique bronze pink color found in the "eye of a partridge".

PRODUCED & BOTTLED BY ALMADÉN VINEYARDS
SAN JOSE, CA BW 145

ALCOHOL 12.5% BY VOLUME • NET CONTENTS 750 ml

PALE
TRIPLE DRY

## ALMADÉN

## VERMOUTH
PALE TRIPLE DRY

PRODUCED AND BOTTLED BY ALMADÉN VINEYARDS
SAN JOSE, CALIFORNIA BW 145
ALCOHOL 18% BY VOLUME

VINTAGE
### 1981
## Laurent Perrier
*CALIFORNIA*
## Chardonnay
*BLANC DE BLANCS*

A brilliant, pale Chardonnay
of delicacy and elegance.
Very dry with unique bouquet
and varietal character.

12%
ALCOHOL
BY VOL.

750 ML
NET
CONTENTS

PRODUCED AND BOTTLED BY
**CAVES LAURENT-PERRIER**
SAN JOSE, CALIF.
BW 145

## ALMADÉN LIGHT

## Light Chablis
### A Dry California Table Wine

48 Calories Per 100 ml. Serving

ALCOHOL 7% BY VOLUME

VINTED & BOTTLED BY ALMADÉN VINEYARDS, SAN JOSE, CA  BW 145

ALMADÉN

*California*
## FLOR FINO SHERRY

A pale, bone-dry Sherry—serve chilled.

MADE AND BOTTLED BY
ALMADÉN VINEYARDS, SAN JOSE, CA BW145
ALCOHOL 17.5% BY VOLUME

*Vineyards Established 1852*

ALMADÉN

*California Solera*
## TINTA TAWNY PORT

A fine Tawny Port made in California from the Tinta
Madeira grape, blended in the Almadén Solera.

MADE AND BOTTLED BY
ALMADÉN VINEYARDS, SAN JOSE, CA BW145
ALCOHOL 19% BY VOLUME

*Vineyards Established 1852*

Here is
a superb
Tawny Port
which owes its
color—a deep crim-
son touched with autum-
nal brown—to the way it has
been made, aged, and blended.
Traditionally, a Tawny Port is one
that has been matured in small oak
barrels which are never empty and
in which younger wines are blended
with older wines of
the same character
and type.

Almaden
Tawny Port
has gone through
a similar process—
the Almaden Solera
System. It was made pri-
marily from the Tinta Madei-
ra grape which originates in Portugal,
but is grown in California. The softness and elegant finish—sweet, yet
not cloying—plus the rich bouquet
and taste of this fine
wine are all evidence
of the care with which
it has been made.

0   80120 61301

Below: Pruned vines on the slopes of the David Bruce Winery in the Santa Cruz Mountains. Bottom: 'Something attempted, something done' at the David Bruce Winery.

**Brookside Vineyard,** Guasti, San Bernardino, Ca.
Now owned by a Chicago food company this winery was founded at the beginning of the century by an Italian immigrant named Secondo Guasti. Its best wines are sold under the brand name Assumption Abbey.

**David Bruce Winery,** 21439 Bear Creek Road, Los Gatos, Ca 95030.
The winery takes its name from its founder, a doctor practicing dermatology in the Santa Clara Valley in South California. This was in 1964 when he built the winery in the Santa Cruz Mountains. He still works there but now has a full-time winemaker and Manager Keith D Hohlfeldt. Bruce began with an interest in the Pinot Noir grape but this has now widened considerably and the vineyard grows Chardonnay and White Riesling as well, all yielding estate-bottled wines. Other wines are mostly from grapes from other vineyards such as Zinfandel from El Dorado County, northwest of Sacramento, and Cabernet Sauvignon and Petite Sirah from San Luis Obispo County, 200 miles south of San Francisco. The winery also makes a popular non-vintage red and white wine called Old Dog.

**California Growers Winery,** Fresno, Ca.
As its name indicates, a cooperative concern nearly 50 years old. It produces mainly straightforward wines, both still and sparkling, and more recently some premium varietals.

**Callaway Vineyard,** Riverside, Temecula, Ca.
Situated about half way between Los Angeles and San Diego and some 60 miles north of the Mexican border this is one of the most southerly of the California wineries. Nevertheless under winemaker Stephen O'Donnell it produces wines of quality — Chardonnay, Chenin Blanc, Fumé Blanc, Sauvignon Blanc, Cabernet Sauvignon, Petite Sirah and Zinfandel. Also Sweet Nancy, a Chenin Blanc and Noel, a Zinfandel.

**East Side Winery,** Lodi, San Joaquin Valley, Ca.
This is another cooperative nearly 50 years old. Its estate-bottled wines, that is, grown and bottled at the winery, include : in reds, Gold and Ruby Cabernet; in whites, Chenin Blanc, Emerald Riesling, Gray Riesling and Sémillon.

**Franzia Brothers,** Escalon, San Joaquin Valley, Ca.
Only some 45 miles east of Yosemite National Park this is another winery owned by the Coca-Cola Company. It is huge with a 20,000,000 gallons capacity and produces modest wines in bulk.

**E & J Gallo,** Modesto, Ca.
Modesto is not a very appropriate address for this huge concern with a capacity of 200,000,000 gallons of wine, a winery that looks from the air like a Middle East oil depot, and a consumer of grapes annually from an estimated 100,000 acres of vineyards in all parts of California. The beginnings were modest enough. The E and J stand for Ernest and John, sons of an Italian immigrant who owned a small vineyard at Modesto. Not many present-day wine moguls can claim that they used mules to work their vineyards, but the Gallo brothers did for although they had a tractor they could not afford the gas to use it. In 1933, following the repeal of Prohibition, they seized the opportunity to make their own wine instead of only growing grapes, managed to raise $5,900.23 capital, rented a railroad shed for $60 a month, and bought a grape crusher and redwood tanks on credit. Not knowing anything about making wine they consulted the author of a pamphlet on winemaking who turned

out to be a Professor at the University of California. At first they produced wine in bulk for local bottlers and they did not bottle under their own label until 1943. A few years later they began to explore the possibilities of varietal grapes, planting and replanting over 400 different varieties in their experimental vineyard in the 1950s and 1960s. Gallo's wines are not made at Modesto and in a way the concern operates on the basis of individual wineries working under the general direction of Julio Gallo. Some are owned by Gallo and others work under their supervision. Thus Napa Valley grapes are crushed under Gallo supervision at the Napa Valley Cooperative Winery, those from Sonoma and Mendocino Counties at the Gallo Winery in the Dry Creek Valley and those from Monterey in Gallo's Livingstone Winery. Still a privately-owned family business Gallo does not disguise the fact that it caters for the popular, bulk wine market, including Champagne by the Charmat process, but it does produce some premium wines – Chablis Blanc, French Colombard, Chenin Blanc are examples, and there are plans to produce more.

**Guild Wine Company,** Lodi, Ca.
Another bulk-producing giant of still and sparkling wines with a 60,000,000 gallons capacity. Its Vino de Tavola, a semisweet red, is a best seller.

**Lamont Winery,** San Joaquin Valley, Ca.
Another giant (owned by Canada's Labatt Brewery) with a production capacity of 60,000,000 gallons, producing still and sparkling wines in bulk. Some premium wines are sold under a M Lamont label.

**Paul Masson Vineyards,** 13150 Saratoga Avenue, Saratoga, Ca 95070.
Another of the giants of the industry and the biggest exporter of wines from the United States, this winery has been since 1943 a subsidiary of the Seagram Company. Before that it had also enjoyed a high reputation in the hands of Paul Masson who gave the concern its name. It was the destruction wrought in France by phylloxera

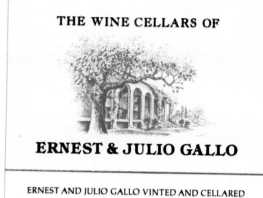

Right: The imposing entrance to the Paul Masson Mountain Winery at Saratoga.

Below: Rows of vines in the famous Paul Masson Pinnacles Vineyard in the Salinas Valley. The rows go due east.

on his family vineyard that brought the 19-year-old French boy to California. While studying at the University of the Pacific at Santa Clara he met a compatriot who had married the daughter of an established wine grower, also French, who had inherited his vineyards. Masson married their daughter, planted his own vineyards in the hills above Saratoga and these were increased when he inherited his father-in-law's. Paul Masson himself, who became a well-known and popular Californian character, retired in 1936 four years before his death aged 81, having firmly established the reputation of the winery which as early as 1900 had won an award for its Champagne at the Paris Exposition. Today the firm harvests 4,464 acres in Monterey County. Its Pinnacles Vineyard at Soledad, with its near 11,000,000-gallon storage capacity winery, produces vintage-dated, estate-bottled premium wines of distinction. Masson has three other wineries – the Champagne and Wine Cellars in Saratoga storing nearly 6,000,000 gallons and with a bottling capacity of 8,000,000 cases a year: the Paul Masson Sherry Cellars in Madera with a 866,000-gallon oak barrel aging cellar and 16,000,000-gallon storage capacity; and Wine Aging and Distribution Center in San Jose. The soil of the Monterey County vineyard is composed of shallow clay loams consisting of decomposed granite washed down from the Gavilan Mountains and sandy loams. These soils, gravelly and low in lime content, have been compared with those of the vineyards of the Médoc in Bordeaux. There are now 22 varieties of grapes flourishing in the Pinnacles Vineyards including Chardonnay, Cabernet Sauvignon, Pinot Noir, Johannisberg Riesling and Gewürztraminer as well as varieties developed by the University of California, Davis, as being ideally suited to the local conditions, notably Emerald Riesling and Flora. Joseph Stillman has been Paul Masson's winemaker for 20 years and the first of the Pinnacles selection, vintage-dated, estate-bottled wines were released in 1976. Stillman releases as Pinnacles selections (that is, Chardonnay, Johannisberg Riesling, Gewürztraminer and Fumé Blanc) only those wines which meet the highest standards. Thus its estate-bottled Champagne made from a cuvée of 100 percent Johannisberg Riesling was released from the 1974 and 1976 vintages but not from the 1975. But as the astronomical figures already mentioned show not all Masson's wines are fine premium wines. They are unashamedly makers of popular, moderately priced wines for the masses. They export to 50 countries and their carafes of California Red and White wines are as familiar a sight in, for example, British supermarkets as they are in United States stores. Here is not the place to list all their products for they make 47 types of table, dessert, apéritif and sparkling wines as well as brandy. To choose a few there are the Pinnacles Selection estate-bottled Chardonnay and Fumé Blanc (from Sauvignon Blanc grapes) and Gewürztraminer, Cabernet

Above: The heavy bunches of Pinot grapes ready for picking.

Left: Harvesting at the Pinnacles Vineyard.

Right: Three of Paul Masson's popular carafe wines.

Below: Three varietals.

PAUL MASSON.
*California Rosé Wine*

A medium-sweet and fruity wine with a fine bouquet and typical rich rose-pink color. Paul Masson Rosé is an all-occasion wine which can be served by itself— as an aperitif—or to accompany main courses. Serve chilled. Produce of U.S.A. Produced and Bottled by Paul Masson Vineyards, Saratoga, California, U.S.A. 11.5% Vol.

1 Litre (e)

*California*
ZINFANDEL
*Full-Bodied and Dry*

A fine, hearty, full-bodied wine—deep red in color. One of the most versatile of red wines, Paul Masson's Zinfandel is a perfect companion to most dinner entrees. Serve at room temperature.

PAUL MASSON.

Alc. 12% by Vol. • Paul Masson Vineyards, Saratoga, Ca., U.S.A. • Contents 75 cl (e)

*California*
PINOT CHARDONNAY

The shy-bearing and delicate Pinot Chardonnay—one of the finest white wine grapes—produces this California wine. It is full and well-balanced, with a rich bouquet and a distinct varietal character. Serve well chilled.

PAUL MASSON.

11.5% Vol.        Produced & bottled by Paul Masson Vineyards, Saratoga, Ca., U.S.A.  Product of U.S.A.        75 cl (e)

California Emerald

*A crisp, medium dry, white wine.
Serve well chilled.*

PAUL MASSON.

Produced and Bottled by Paul Masson Vineyards, Saratoga, California, U.S.A.
11% Vol.    75 cl (e)    Product of U.S.A.

Sauvignon, Zinfandel, Pinot Noir, Pinot Chardonnay, California Rosé, California Emerald (a crisp, dry white), and California Sparkling Wine, fermented in the bottle. Like that old-established California winery, Buena Vista, in the Sonoma Valley, Paul Masson's is a minor cultural center. In the outdoor amphitheater adjoining the winery 'Music at the Vineyards,' a series of summer concerts of classical music has been a feature for a quarter of a century together with concerts of folk, jazz and blues, performances of Shakespeare and other events.

**Mirassou Vineyards,** Santa Clara, Ca.
The name Mirassou is closely associated with the development of varietal grapes in southern California and now with the production of high-quality premium wines. Its 1,000 acres of vineyards in Santa Clara and in Monterey, the latter close to those of Masson, enable them to produce a score of wines including notably a Sylvaner Riesling and a White Riesling, a Cabernet Sauvignon, Gamay Beaujolais and Zinfandel.

**The Monterey Vineyard,** 800 South Alta St, Gonzales, Cal.
Upper Monterey County where this winery is situated has an unusually long growing season with the vine buds breaking in February, sometimes earlier, and the grapes being harvested as late as November, even later. The vineyard has been owned since

The Mediterranean-style winery of the Monterey Vineyard at Gonzales.

Left: A woman assistant checking storage barrels at the Monterey Vineyard.

Above: Tasting at the Monterey Vineyard.

1977 by a subsidiary of the Coca-Cola Company of America and its winemaker is Dr Richard Peterson, one of the most distinguished figures in the wine industry and a former Supreme Knight of the Universal Order of Knights of the Vine. His interest in wine — he was for 10 years with E and J Gallo where he became Research Director — is being handed down, for his eldest daughter is a graduate in Enology from the University of California at Davis where his youngest is also studying enology. Under Dr Peterson's direction the vineyard produces a wide selection of sound varietals and is organized so that wines can be produced in very small lots thus encouraging an innovative approach. Outstanding are its Special Signature wines (so called because the labels carry the winemaker's signature) and its Classic wines. The Special Signatures are: Thanksgiving Harvest Johannisberg Riesling produced from botrytis ('noble rot') affected grapes; Botrytis Sauvignon Blanc, which can develop in the bottle for 10 years or more; and December Harvest Zinfandel, matured in small oak barrels. The Classics are: Classic California Red, from a blend of Cabernet Sauvignon, Zinfandel and Pinot Noir; Classic California Dry White from Pinot Blanc, Chenin Blanc, French Colombard and Gray Riesling; and Classic California Rosé from Grenache, Cabernet Sauvignon, Napa Gamay, Gray Riesling and Pinot Noir. Other wines include: Chardonnay, Pinot Blanc, Johannisberg Riesling, Chenin Blanc, Monterey County Riesling, Soft White Riesling, Gumer Sylvaner, Fumé Blanc, Rosé Cabernet Sauvignon, Rosé of Pinot Noir, Zinfandel, Pinot Noir and Petite Sirah.

**Ridge Vineyards,** 17100 Monte Bello Road, Cupertino, Ca.
Despite its high reputation this winery on the whole is a modest affair. Its 50-acre vineyard stands magnificently 2,500 feet above the Pacific Ocean in the Santa Cruz Mountains and, of course, is too small to provide for the 40–45,000 cases that the winery produces annually. In fact its grapes — the Monte Bello vineyard is planted almost entirely with Cabernet Sauvignon — come from far and wide, brought by truck up the mountain road from other vineyards, some as far as 200 miles away.

Like so many California wine ventures it began as an amateur affair. It was in the early 1960s that four electronics engineers from Stanford Research Institute nearby thought it would be a good idea to make wine in their spare time and acquired the lofty vineyard which had been in fact a rather unremarkable vineyard for some 60 years. At first they produced over 5,000 gallons a year but then decided that they needed a full-time winemaker and engaged Paul Draper, the present winemaker and a fervent admirer of Bordeaux wines. Under his guidance and that of David Bennion, who is now President of the company but acted as the first winemaker in the 1960s, the annual output has increased to its present level and the reputation of its wines has increased with it. Paul Draper is a believer in the virtues of oak barrels for aging, and American oak at that. The winery's products, mostly red, include Monte Bello Cabernet Sauvignon, Zinfandel York Creek, Petite Sirah and Chardonnay.

**Turgeon and Lohr Winery,** 1000 Lenzen Avenue, San Jose, Ca 95126.
One of Southern California's new wineries – its first grapes were planted in Monterey County in 1972 – it is already producing distinctive wines of character. The original plantings were at Greenfield in Monterey County where the winery has 280 acres of rich loamy soil over a deep base of river-run gravel. Here they grow Chardonnay, Pinot Blanc, Sauvignon Blanc, Johannisberg Riesling, Gamay, Zinfandel and Pinot Noir grapes. In a smaller vineyard some 150 miles north in the Sacramento Valley Delta they grow Chenin Blanc and Petite Sirah which were not a success in the more southern area but flourish here. Turgeon and Lohr concentrate on table wines and believe strongly that wine's association with food should be constantly kept in mind. Their wines include Sacramento County Chenin Blanc, Northern California Petite Sirah, Northern California Trois Cuvées Cabernet Sauvignon (all these from the Delta area). Those labeled Monterey include Johannisberg Riesling, Chardonnay, Pinot Blanc, Sauvignon Blanc, Gamay, Pinot Noir, Rosé, Cabernet Sauvignon, Fumé Blanc, Rosé Wine Selection, and Jade, a low-alcohol content white wine.

CHAPTER FOUR

# North Western States

WASHINGTON

IDAHO
OREGON

## WASHINGTON

Twenty years ago no one would have associated the State of Washington, most northerly of the western States, with the production of wine. Today this is not the case. Washington ranks third in the United States in the production of grapes and has about 4,000 acres planted with *vinifera* grapes with more planned. It has over 20 wineries of one sort or another, some it must be admitted, small and very new and therefore untried.

The principal grape-growing area is in the Yakima Valley in the Columbia Plateau in the south of the State. The Columbia Plateau is part of the largest lava plateau in the world. The Yakima River rises in the Cascade Mountains west of the plateau and flows into the Columbia River of which it is a tributary near Pasco on the northern side of Horse Heaven Hills. It is in this area that most of the vineyards are to be found although there are some situated much further north in the neighborhood of Seattle. Most northerly and newest – their first crush was scheduled for 1982 – are the Mount Baker Vineyards at Deming only some 10 miles from the Canadian border.

Washington, like other states such as Ohio and Michigan, is typical of the resurgence of interest in wine and its production in North America. As has been said all the wineries and vineyards have sprung up in the last 25 years or so, many in the past five or six. Many are one-man or husband and wife concerns and sometimes winemaking though commercial is only a part-time activity. One winery in Walla Walla (which sounds more like Australia than North America) is operated from a small shed behind the owner's house but produces a Cabernet Sauvignon and a Merlot which are well spoken of and sell quickly. Some wineries, not surprisingly have not yet produced any wine at all but they are there and will. As might be expected with such recent plantings the grapes grown are mostly European *vinifera* types – Chardonnays, Cabernet Sauvignon, Rieslings, Merlots etc.

Previous page: Cloudy skies over the Yakima Valley.

Left: Cabernet grapes on the Hinzerling vineyard.

96

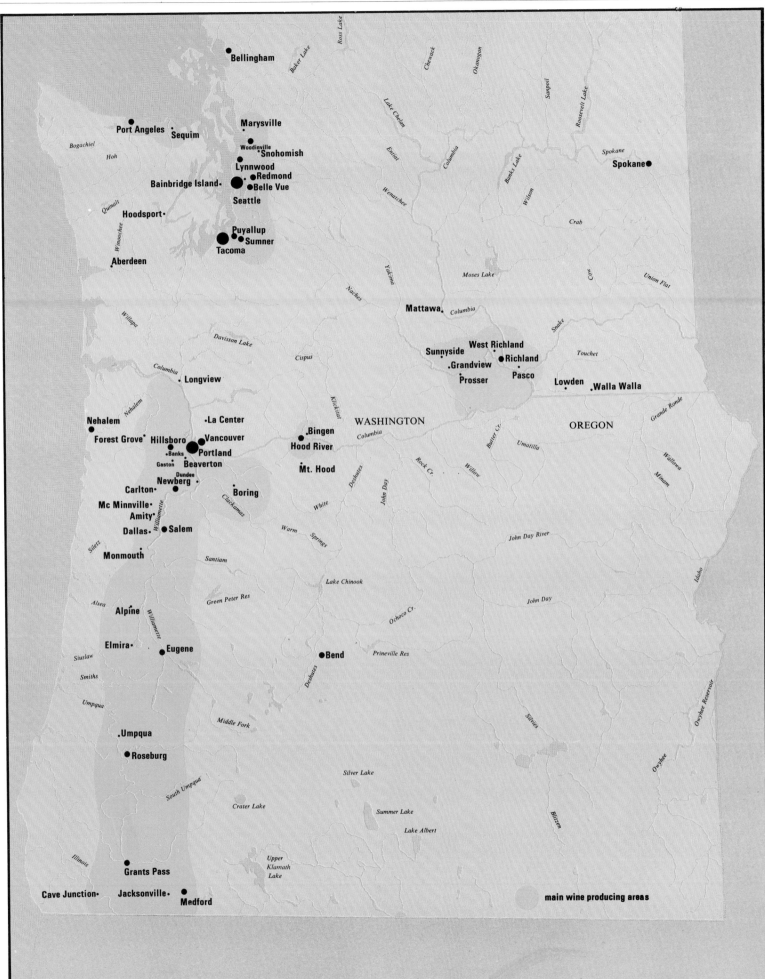

Bellingham

Port Angeles
Sequim

Marysville
Woodinville
Snohomish
Lynnwood
Redmond
Bainbridge Island·
Belle Vue
Seattle

Hoodsport·

Puyallup
Sumner
Tacoma

Aberdeen

*Bogachiel*
*Hoh*
*Quinalt*
*Winooskee*

*Ross Lake*
*Baker Lake*

*Chewack*
*Okanogan*
*Sanpoil*

*Lake Chelan*
*Entiat*
*Columbia*
*Banks Lake*
*Wilson*
*Roosevelt Lake*

*Spokane*
Spokane●

*Wenatchee*
*Crab*

*Naches*
*Yakima*
*Moses Lake*
*Cox*
*Union Flat*

Mattawa.
*Columbia*

*Davisson Lake*

*Willapa*

Longview
*Columbia*

*Cispus*

West Richland
Sunnyside
Richland
Grandview
Pasco
Prosser
Lowden
·Walla Walla

*Touchet*
*Snake*

Nehalem
Forest Grove·
Hillsboro·
·La Center
Vancouver
·Bingen
Hood River

WASHINGTON
*Columbia*

OREGON
*Grande Ronde*

·Banks
Gaston·
Portland
Beaverton
Dundee
Newberg
Carlton·
Mc Minnville
Amity·
Dallas·
Salem

Boring
Mt. Hood

*Nehalem*
*Klickitat*
*Deschutes*
*Rock Cr.*
*Willow*
*Umatilla*

*Minam*
*Wallowa*

Monmouth

*Siletz*
*Willamette*
*Santiam*
*Clackamas*
*White*
*Warm*
*Springs*
*John Day*

*John Day River*
*John Day*

*Idaho*

Alpine
*Alsea*
*Willamette*

Elmira·
Eugene●

●Bend
*Prineville Res*
*Ochoco Cr.*
*Lake Chinook*

*Siuslaw*
*Smiths*
*Umpqua*
*Middle Fork*
*Deschutes*
*Silvies*

*Owyhee Reservoir*

·Umpqua

Roseburg

*Silver Lake*

*South Umpqua*

*Crater Lake*
*Summer Lake*
*Lake Albert*

*Owyhee*
*Blitzen*

*Illinois*
Grants Pass

Cave Junction·
Jacksonville·
Medford

*Upper*
*Klamath*
*Lake*

**main wine producing areas**

**Associated Vintners,** 3468 150th Avenue, NE Redmond, Wa 98052.
At the northern end of Lake Sommamish, 10 miles east of Seattle, this vineyard was planted in 1963 and made its first varietal wine in 1967. Their wines today are almost entirely varietals. In whites they produce Gewürztraminer, Johannisberg Riesling, Chardonnay and Sémillon with occasionally a blend named Valley White. In reds they rely on Cabernet Sauvignon and Pinot Noir.

**Bingen Wine Cellars (Mont Elise Vineyards),** 315 West Steuben, Bingen, Wa. 98605. Southernmost of the Washington wineries it lies on the Oregon border in the Columbia River Gorge. It is owned by the Charles Henderson family who tested out varieties of *vinifera* grapes from 1966 onward and started the winery in 1975. It now has a storage capacity of 14,000 gallons and produces from its Mont Elise vineyards Pinot Noir and Gewürztraminer, and from the Don Graves vineyard, 17 miles away, Chenin Blanc and Grenache.

**Chateau Ste Michelle,** Woodinville, Wa 98072.
This is one of the oldest and perhaps the most prestigious of the Washington wineries. Its 750 acres of vineyards in the Yakima Valley are planted with Cabernet Sauvignon, Pinot Noir, Sémillon, Johannisberg Riesling, Chenin Blanc, Merlot, Grenache, Chardonnay and Gewürztraminer vines and the 'château' housing the 160,000 square feet winery, standing in 87 acres of beautiful grounds is, if not exactly a

The handsome winery of Chateau Ste Michelle at Woodinville built in 1912.

Chateau Ste Michelle
WASHINGTON STATE
MUSCAT ALEXANDRIA
1980

Produced and Bottled by Ste. Michelle Vineyards Bonded Winery #8
Woodinville, Washington  Alcohol 11½% by Volume

VINTAGE 1978

Chateau Ste. Michelle ®
*Washington State*

CABERNET SAUVIGNON

Produced and Bottled by Ste. Michelle Vineyards
Woodinville, Wash. Alcohol 12½% by Volume

château, a handsome manor house built in 1912. The Château's first harvest of premium wines was as recent as 1967. The soil of the vineyards is sandy loam on a rocky volcanic base and the winery claims that this, combined with optimal climatic conditions and freedom from disease bring near ideal growing conditions. The vineyards, incidentally, lie on the same latitude as the Bordeaux and Burgundy regions of France. Among the winery's special products, their enologist special consultant is the distinguished Andre Tchelistcheff, are a Blanc de Noir made by the *méthode Champenoise* and a Johannisberg Riesling made from late harvested botrytized grapes. Other wines include Chenin Blanc, Fumé Blanc, Sémillon Blanc, Gewürztraminer, Muscat Canelli, Chardonnay, Grenache Rosé, Rosé of Cabernet, Merlot and Cabernet Sauvignon.

The sandy loam soil of the 750-acre Chateau Ste Michelle vineyard.

99

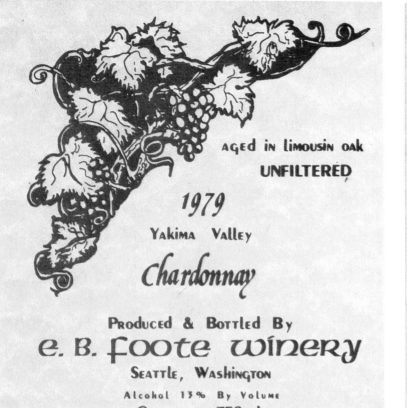

AGED IN LIMOUSIN OAK
UNFILTERED

1979

Yakima Valley

*Chardonnay*

PRODUCED & BOTTLED BY

e. B. foote winery

SEATTLE, WASHINGTON

Alcohol 13% By Volume
CONTENTS 750 mL.

UNFILTERED

1979

Yakima Valley

*Gewürztraminer*

PRODUCED & BOTTLED BY

e. B. foote winery

SEATTLE, WASHINGTON

Alcohol 13% By Volume
CONTENTS 750 mL.

**E B Foote Winery,** 3836 34th Avenue, SW Seattle, Wa 98126.
The Footes, owners of this modest winery believe (as do those of the Preston Wine Cellars) that the local grapes they use to make their wines are equal to any grape produced in the world. They, too, are one of Washington's newest wine concerns — their first crush of 1,000 gallons was in 1978 — but they are already producing a Chardonnay and a Gewürztraminer both of which have won prizes in local competitions. The winemaker and owner is Gene Foote who in his spare time is a full-time senior engineer with the Boeing Company — or perhaps that should be the other way round. He is assisted in the winery by his wife and sons, one of whom is completing a degree course in enology at the University of California, Davis, and between them they managed to produce 4,000 gallons of wine in 1981, double the previous year's production. The winery is in a small industrial park in Seattle itself and the Footes do not grow their own grapes but use the produce of growers in the Yakima Valley.

**Hinzerling Vineyards,** 1520 Sheridan Avenue, Prosser, Wa.
The vineyard lies on the north side of the Yakima Valley, about six miles north of Prosser in the southern part of the State. It was planted in 1972 by the Wallace family who operate the business, with White Riesling, Gewürztraminer, Chardonnay, Merlot and Cabernet Sauvignon grapes and the first pressing was in 1976. The winery specializes in the production of sweet wines resulting from botrytis ('noble rot') which affects the late ripening White Riesling and Gewürztraminer grapes. Michael Wallace, the enologist of the family, who signs the labels, gives a remarkably detailed account on them of the processes involved in making the different wines including the quantity produced. The wines include: Washington Merlot; Die Sonne, a botrytis wine from cluster Gewürztraminer grapes; Yakima Valley Late Harvest White Riesling, another botrytis wine; Cabernet Sauvignon; Chardonnay; Ashfall White; Gewürztraminer; Washington Cabernet Sauvignon blended with Merlot.

**Neuharth Winery Inc,** Sequim, Wa.
For a short while, it was started only in 1978, this was the most northerly winery on the West coast of the United States, but that honor now goes to Mount Baker Vineyards at Deming which made its first crush in 1982. Eugene and Marie Neuharth — he had previously worked in California vineyards — established their winery at

Right: Loading must to press at the Hinzerling Vineyard.

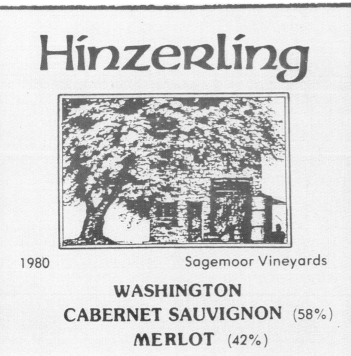

Hinzerling

1980          Sagemoor Vineyards

**WASHINGTON**
**CABERNET SAUVIGNON** (58%)
**MERLOT** (42%)

Produced and Bottled by Hinzerling Vineyards, Prosser, WA.
Alcohol 12.5% by Volume

Hinzerling
Vineyards

Ashfall White

Yakima Valley    1981    Table Wine

Produced & bottled by Hinzerling Vineyards, Prosser, Washington
Alcohol 12% by Volume

Above: The Hinzerling Vineyards in the Yakima Valley in southern Washington.

Right: Gewürztraminer grapes from the Hinzerling vineyard.

Eugene and Marie Neuharth bottling at their own winery.

Sequim in a log pole dairy barn, filling it with stainless-steel vats, American oak barrels etc. Sequim is about 40 miles north of Seattle. The winery, which has had cellars added, is designed to cater for a 4,000 gallon per year operation. In 1980, using grapes from elsewhere in the State and from Oregon and California, they produced their first wines. These were Johannisberg Riesling, Chenin Blanc, White Zinfandel and Zinfandel. Since then they have added Cabernet Sauvignon, Dungeness White, made from Riesling grapes and aged in oak, Dungeness Red and Dungeness Rosé. The Neuharths are experimenting with a small vineyard near the winery in the hope of finding a suitable strain that will flourish there.

**Preston Wine Cellars,** Star Route, Box 1234, Pasco, Wa 99301.
Can it be true that any winery does not have a care? It must be for Preston Wine Cellars' cellarmaster is actually named Tom Sans Souci. Robert Griffin is the wine-maker and a graduate in Enology at the University of California at Davis. He is responsible to Bill and Joann Preston for producing premium wines from the winery's 180 acres of vineyards at Pasco on the Columbia River in the south of the State, just about 100 miles south of the Coulée Dam. The Prestons started with a 50-acre vineyard in 1972–3 and increased this to 180 acres in 1979. Their first crush, only 190 tons, was in 1976. Their present production is about 60,000 gallons per year and they plan to produce about 150,000 gallons of wine from their own grapes and another 50,000 to 100,000 from grapes purchased elsewhere. Their vineyard is planted with 11 varieties of European *vinifera* – Sauvignon Blanc, Chardonnay, Gewürztraminer, Johannisberg Riesling, Chenin Blanc, Gamay Beaujolais, Pinot Noir, Royalty, Merlot and Muscat of Alexandria. Bill Preston declares without mincing matters, 'We feel we are in the heart of the best wine-grape region in Washington State, and possibly in the world.' The winery, whose prime interest is in wines with the foregoing names, has two proprietary names – Desert Gold, a white wine, and Desert Rosé. Despite its comparative youth Preston Wine Cellars has won a number of awards in local (including Oregon) wine competitions.

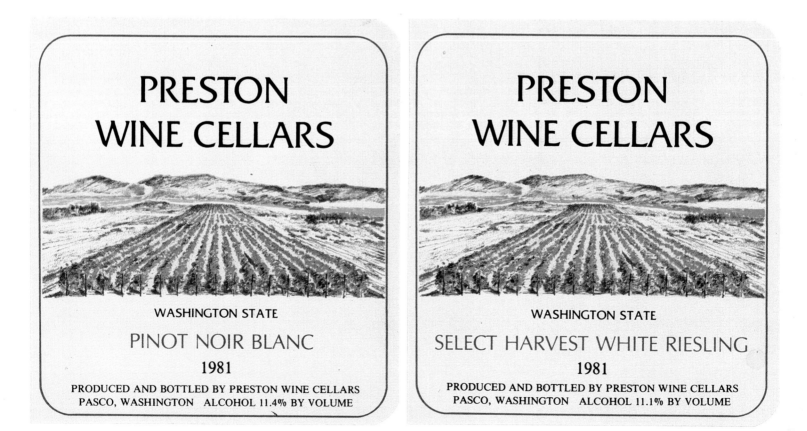

PRESTON WINE CELLARS

WASHINGTON STATE

PINOT NOIR BLANC

1981

PRODUCED AND BOTTLED BY PRESTON WINE CELLARS
PASCO, WASHINGTON   ALCOHOL 11.4% BY VOLUME

PRESTON WINE CELLARS

WASHINGTON STATE

SELECT HARVEST WHITE RIESLING

1981

PRODUCED AND BOTTLED BY PRESTON WINE CELLARS
PASCO, WASHINGTON   ALCOHOL 11.1% BY VOLUME

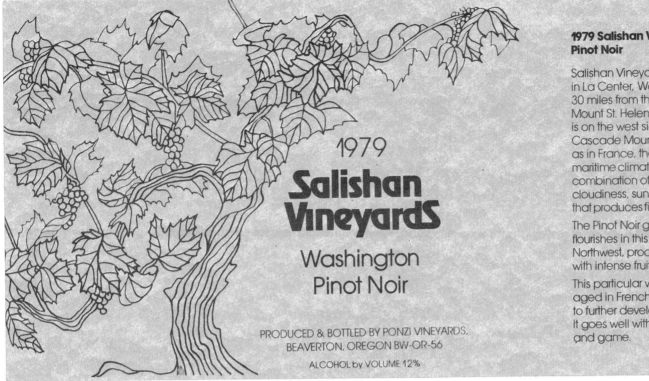

**1979 Salishan Vineyards Pinot Noir**

Salishan Vineyards is located in La Center, Washington, 30 miles from the volcano, Mount St. Helens. The vineyard is on the west side of the Cascade Mountains, where, as in France, the moderate, maritime climate produces that combination of rainfall, cloudiness, sunshine and heat that produces fine wine grapes.

The Pinot Noir grape especially flourishes in this part of the Northwest, producing a wine with intense fruit flavors.

This particular wine has been aged in French Oak barrels to further develop its character. It goes well with all red meats and game.

1979
**Salishan Vineyards**
Washington
Pinot Noir

PRODUCED & BOTTLED BY PONZI VINEYARDS, BEAVERTON, OREGON BW-OR-56

ALCOHOL by VOLUME 12%

**Salishan Vineyards,** Route 2, Box 8, La Center, Wa 98629.
Journalists have been known to be not unenthusiastic consumers of wine but not many have engaged in making it commercially. Lincoln and Joan Fielman are exceptions. They met while both were working on the *Seattle Times* but the interest in winemaking rose from Lincoln's service in the US Army in France when, in a comparative computer study of 50 years of weather conditions at Portland international airport, he discovered similarities with those of French wine-growing regions. He acquired the Salishan Vineyards on the west side of the Cascade Mountains, only 30 miles from the volcano of Mount St Helens, which were planted in 1971 and began producing wines in 1976. Joan is the winemaker and produces Pinot Noir, Cabernet Sauvignon, Riesling and Chenin Blanc.

**Manfred Vierthaler Winery,** 17136 State Hwy, 410 Sumner, Wa 98390.
Just south of Seattle in the Puyallup River Valley the winery was founded in 1976 and is housed in a handsome building reminiscent of the Bavarian Alps on El-Hi-Hill. Manfred Vierthaler, owner and winemaker, follows the traditional German method of winemaking from *vinifera* grape varieties grown in California as well as Washington. He specializes in late-harvest wines from White Riesling and Muller-Thurgau grapes.

Other Washington wineries opened in the past few years are:
**Bainbridge Island Winery,** 682 State Hwy, 305 NE Bainbridge Island, Wa 98110.
**Cedar Ridge Vintners Inc,** 5226 Snohomish-Macias Rd, Snohomish, Wa, founded 1978.
**Kiona Vineyards Winery,** 211S, 46th W Richland, Wa 99352, founded 1979.
**Leonetti Cellar,** 1321 School Ave, Walla Walla, Wa, founded 1977.
**Lost Mountain Winery,** 730 Lost Mountain Rd, Sequim, Wa 98382, founded 1981.
**Tucker Cellars,** Rt 1 Box 1969, Sunnyside, Wa 98944, founded 1981.
**Woodward Canyon Winery,** Rt 1 Box 387, Lowden, Wa 99360, founded 1981.
**Worden's Washington Winery,** 7217 W 45th, Spokane, Wa 99204, founded 1980.
**Yakima River Winery,** Rt 1 Box 1657, N River Rd, Prosser, Wa, founded 1978.

Salishan Vineyards with the volcano of Mount St Helens billowing smoke.

# IDAHO

This mountainous northwestern state does not look at first sight a likely wine-producing area but it has one flourishing vineyard and winery on the volcanic soil at what is felicitously called Sunny Slope, some nine miles southwest of the town of Caldwell near the Oregon border. The area is perhaps more reminiscent, from its names, of the animal than the vegetable world. Snake River, with its Swan Falls flows past Deer Flat Reservoir in the shadow of the Salmon River Mountains. Idaho had a small wine industry started in the 1860s by a Frenchman named Del Sol but it collapsed with Prohibition and was not revived until the 1970s.

**Ste Chapelle Vineyards Inc,** Route 4, Box 775, Caldwell, Id 83605.
It was in 1971 that the Symms family at Sunny Slope planted Johannisberg Riesling, Pinot Noir, Chardonnay and Cabernet Sauvignon grapes and four years later formed a partnership with Bill Broich, an apple grower and amateur winemaker in Emmet, 30 miles to the north. He and his wife had toured the winemaking countries of Europe two years before and the new operation was named Sainte Chapelle after the chapel of that name in Paris. The first harvest at Sunny Slope was in 1975 and using its grapes within two years Ste Chapelle wines were winning prizes. In 1978 the two concerns were formally merged and the winery moved to Sunny Slope with Bill Broich as winemaker. The present building, inspired by the Ste Chapelle chapel in Paris and portrayed on the labels, was completed in 1979 and in 1981 the winery crushed 120,000 gallons. Phylloxera, by the way, has never affected the vines of the region which are not, therefore, grafted. Ste Chapelle wines, mostly aged in French Limousin oak barrels, include Johannisberg Riesling, Chenin Blanc, Chardonnay, Gewürztraminer, Cabernet Sauvignon, a Blanc de Noir, Merlot and a sweet dessert wine Muscat of Alexandria. The winery uses grapes from nearby Washington State as well as the grapes from its own vineyards.

Below: Aging casks at the Ste Chapelle winery.

Bottom: Harvest time in the vineyard.

# Ste. CHAPELLE VINEYARDS

Non-Vintage
**AMERICAN**

## Muscat of Alexandria

Produced and Bottled by Ste. Chapelle Vineyards
Caldwell, Idaho. BWID-8. Alcohol 12% by Volume.

# Ste. CH.
*Fine Wine*

From the earliest days o
by many and supported
world's great wine grape
discovered around the
sea captain.

The grape was nar
word Muscato in Ital'
secretion of the mu
perfumes. It is also f
as in Muscat grapes

Muscat of Alexa
that evolved throu
different regions
now finally bein
excellent dessert
experienced wi
sweet wines, th
the winemakin

*We strive to n
prolonged chilli
process, is neces
are chilled for c
crystals, a con*

# Ste. CHAPELLE VINEYARDS

**SPECIAL HARVEST**

IDAHO 1981
Johannisberg Riesling

Residual sugar 5.3% by weight
Average sugar 24.4% at harvest

Produced and Bottled by Ste. Chapelle Vineyards
Caldwell, Idaho. BWID-8. Alcohol 9.4% by Volume.

Ste Chapelle winery in the snow.

## OREGON

There is one thing that can be said about wine made in this northwestern State. When you drink it you know what you are drinking. Oregon, in fact, has the strictest regulations regarding the description of wines made there than any of the other states. Whatever they may do in the great wine-producing state of California to the south you cannot name a wine, for example, as a Sauterne, a Chablis, a Burgundy or a Champagne in Oregon. And if you call a wine by its grape name, which is what Oregon winemakers do, the wine must be made from 90 per cent of the grape named. At present US Federal regulations require that only 51 percent need be of the grape named although this is to be increased to 75 percent. Oregon does make special allowance for Cabernet Sauvignon because of the blending that wine made from that grape often requires. But if you drink an Oregon Pinot Noir, and recent events suggest that you will be lucky if you do, you can be certain that it is wine made almost entirely if not entirely from that grape.

The recent event referred to was the fantastic near-triumph in 1980 of the Eyrie Vineyards' 1975 Pinot Noir at a blind tasting of top-class French burgundies and US and other wines of the same type held in, of all places, that revered home of Burgundy, Beaune. The tasting was the sequel to an earlier tasting. The second tasting was organized by one of France's leading wineries, Joseph Drouhin. The French wines entered for the first tasting did so poorly that Drouhin asked for a replay on the grounds that the French wines that had been entered were not of the best quality. So a second blind tasting was organized with Drouhin obviously entering the best he could muster. To his consternation and no doubt to that of the whole French wine industry, although his Chambolle-Musigny 1959 came first it was by such a narrow margin – 70 to 69.8 points – as to make it virtually a tie for the first place with Oregon 1975 Pinot Noir. What is more, third in the ratings was a Chambertin 1961, fourth a Beaune and fifth a Vosne-Romanée 1976. Some of France's most famous wines had been trounced by a virtual upstart not even from California or New York but from a state which nobody associated with wine at all.

The Willamette River rises in the Cascade Mountains and flows into the Columbia River at Portland just before that river empties into the Pacific Ocean. Almost all of Oregon's wineries of any significance, and some it must be said of no significance, lie along its valley. There are one or two in the southeast of the State near the Umpqua River but the main concentration is in the north, curiously closer to Washington than to California. The fact is that the grapes grown in the Willamette Valley are very good which is perhaps not surprising seeing that the State of Washington, only a few miles to the north is now the third biggest grape-growing state in the country and rapidly becoming one of its leading wine producers. The rapid growth of Oregon as a wine state is graphically illustrated by the fact that in 1970 there were only about 85 acres under grapes supplying seven wineries. Today some 2,500 acres supply over 30 wineries. Estimates for 1982 production of wine grapes were 2,500 tons, which was expected to yield some 375,000 gallons of wine. Some of the wineries are small and barely off the ground. Indeed someone described Oregon's wine industry as a cottage industry with too many amateurs. But as the history of the industry shows today's amateur is tomorrow's professional. After all David Lett, founder of the triumphant Eyrie Vineyards, was going to be a dentist until he decided to try his hand at winemaking.

Oregon has a cool, rather short growing season. One wine writer suggests that California has cooler edges of what is essentially a warm climate while Oregon has the warmer edges of what is basically a cool climate.

**Eyrie Vineyards,** 935 E 10th Avenue, McMinnville, Or.
This winery's triumph at the blind tasting in Beaune, France in 1980, reported earlier in this chapter, clearly puts it top of the poll among the Oregon wineries. It was in 1965 that David Lett, owner and winemaker who has a degree in viticulture from the University of California, Davis, arrived in the Willamette Valley and, backing

This is a very limited bottling of
1979 Pinot gris

a dry white table wine grown and bottled by

The Eyrie Vineyards

Winery - McMinnville, Oregon. Vineyards - Dundee, Oregon

Alcohol 12½% by volume

The Eyrie Vineyards looking west from the Red Hills of Dundee. The grapes are one-year-old Pinot Gris.

his belief that Pinot Noir was the right grape for the area, planted 3,000 cuttings of the types grown in Burgundy and Alsace. At the same time he planted a few Chardonnay, Riesling, Gewürztraminer, Muscat Ottonis, Pinot Gris and Pinot Munier. From the last two he now produces about 100 cases each year for special customers. The winery is a converted plant previously used for processing turkeys and his fermenting tanks either plastic-lined hoppers previously used for processing cherries or stainless-steel drums which once contained syrup concentrate for Coca-Cola. Lett has never lost faith in Pinot Noir grapes whose success in California has by no means been great. The climate of the Willamette Valley, he says, is infinitely more suitable than that of the Napa and Sonoma Valleys which, he says, is too hot. So the winery concentrates on its Pinot Noir and its wisdom in doing so certainly seems to be reflected in the 1980 success in Beaune. This, it should be recalled was the 1975 vintage, that is only 10 years after the winery started. Besides the Pinot Noir and the Pinot Gris and Pinot Munier already mentioned, Eyrie Vineyards produce an Oregon Chardonnay, a Gewürztraminer and an unusual, strongly flavored Muscat Ottonal.

**Hinman Vineyards,** 27012 Briggs Hill Road, Eugene, Or 97405.
This is one of the newest of the Oregon wineries. It was in 1972 that Doyle Hinman, trained in Geisenheim, Germany, began planting 10 acres of land with Pinot Noir and later Riesling, Chardonnay and Gewürztraminer grapes and the first wines from this were due on the market in 1982. A second nine-acre vineyard was planted in 1980 with Riesling, Pinot Noir and Gewürztraminer and its first harvest is due in 1983. The winery produced over 2,700 cases of wine in 1980, slightly less in 1981, but aims at 9,000 cases in the future. Its present wines include: Riesling, Gewürztraminer, White Cabernet, Chardonnay, White Pinot, Pinot Noir, Cabernet Sauvignon. The winery is owned by a partnership of the Hinman and Smith families.

Preparing the Hinman vineyards.

Weighing up at the end of the day.

Into the Hinman press.

**Knudsen-Erath**, Dundee, Or.
Wines produced include Yamhill County Vintage Select and Yamhill County Estate-Bottled, both Pinot Noir, Chardonnay, White Riesling and under Dundee Villages labels, reds and whites.

**Oak Knoll Winery**, route 6 Box 184, Hillsborough, Or.
As the labels suggest Oak Knoll began with fruit and berry wines but its owners Ron and Marjorie Vuylsteke have moved into the field of vinifera wines and have

111

**Oak Knoll**

OREGON
RHUBARB
WINE

*A light, dry, delicate wine with a natural tartness*

**OREGON BONDED WINERY NO. 50**
PRODUCED & BOTTLED BY OAK KNOLL WINERY, INC. HILLSBORO, OR

ALCOHOL 12½% BY VOLUME

**Oak Knoll**

OREGON
BLACKBERRY
WINE

*A rich, zesty wine with a hint of sweetness*

**OREGON BONDED WINERY NO. 50**
PRODUCED & BOTTLED BY OAK KNOLL WINERY, INC. HILLSBORO, OR

ALCOHOL 12½% BY VOLUME

VINTAGE 1981
OREGON
GEWURZTRAMINER

**Oak Knoll**

*A spicy aromatic white wine with a fruity flavor*

OREGON BONDED WINERY NO. 50
PRODUCED & BOTTLED BY OAK KNOLL WINERY, INC. HILLSBORO, OR

ALCOHOL 12½% BY VOLUME

won local awards for their white Riesling and Pinot Noir. Their varietals, including Chardonnay and Sauvignon Blanc, are marketed under the label Château de Chene — Chene being the French for oak and in this case Château is perhaps winery. The winery depends for its grapes on independent grape growers. It has produced as much as 10,000 gallons a year but cut this back to 4,000 gallons in 1981.

The Vuylstekes are now experimenting with the native North American Niagara Grape.

**Siskiyou Vineyards,** 6220 Caves Highway, Cave Junction, Or 97523.
The most southerly of the Oregon vineyards for Cave Junction, in the Illinois River Valley, is less than 20 miles from the north California State line. It is run by a woman, Mrs Carol J David, widow of the joint founder and it was she who designed the new winery. The business is a small affair, the vineyard extending for only 12 acres and originally (it was started in 1974) the winery was in the basement of the owners' house. Today the new winery contains offices, an enology laboratory and storage facilities for 15,000 gallons in stainless-steel tanks and French Limousin oak barrels. It produces Cabernet Sauvignon, Pinot Noir, Merlot, Gewürztraminer, White Riesling and Sémillon and is clearly firmly established.

**Sokol Blosser Winery,** PO Box 199, Blanchard Lane, Dundee, Or 97115.
It was in 1971 that Phil Blosser and his wife Susan Sokol Blosser began planting their vineyards. It was at weekends because both had jobs, he as an environmental planner, she as a professor of history. They had 100 acres of fruit trees in the Red Hills of Dundee in the Willamette Valley, some 20 miles from Portland and of these they have converted 45 acres to vineyards; 15 acres are under Chardonnay, 14 under White Riesling and 13 under Pinot Noir as the principal varieties with Cabernet Sauvignon, Merlot and Muller-Thurgau in the rest. The winery itself, built to order, started up in 1976 and then the Blossers engaged a winemaker, Dr Bob McRitchie, a chemist, who had been with Franciscan Vineyards in the Napa Valley. Today the winery has a production capacity of 55,000 gallons annually and this was achieved as early as 1980 and 1981. Its wines have already achieved remarkable successes in wine competitions including Gold, Silver and Bronze Medals in London. Their Chardonnay and Pinot Noir are aged in traditional Limousin oak barrels, the lighter whites in temperature-controlled stainless-steel tanks. Sokol Blosser produce a Johannisberg Riesling, Chardonnay, Pinot Noir, Gewürztraminer, Sauvignon Blanc (Fumé Blanc), Rosé, Muller-Thurgau, Merlot and Bouquet Blanc.

**Tualatin Vineyards,** Route 1, Box 339, Forest Grove, Or 97116.
This vineyard, beautifully situated amid orchards and Douglas fir with the snow-capped peak of Mount Hood 60 miles away visible on clear days, extends for 80 acres and was originally planted, at least 65 acres were, in 1973–75 with White Riesling, Chardonnay, Gewürztraminer and Pinot Noir. The vines are trained high on trellises to capture full sunlight and air exposure and the winery harvests about 160 tons which yield about 8,500 cases. Eventual targets are 250 tons or 15,000 cases annually and meanwhile Tualatin buys quality grapes from selected growers both in Oregon and nearby Washington State. As might be expected from the youth of the winery most of the equipment is modern, including stainless-steel tanks and refrigerator equipment, but there are also traditional small French oak aging barrels, all housed in an old converted strawberry packing shed covering 14,000 square feet. Tualatin (from a local Indian word meaning 'gentle or easy flowing' but referring to a local river and not the wine) was started in 1972 by Bill Malkmus and Bill Fuller. The latter, holder of a Master's degree in Enology from the University of California, Davis, once in charge of wine production at Louis M Martini in the Napa Valley, is the winemaker and Bill Malkmuss looks after the business side. They believe that the wines best suited to Oregon conditions are White Riesling, Gewürztraminer, Chardonnay and Pinot Noir and it is on these that they concentrate. They also make small quantities of Sauvignon Blanc, Early Muscat and Pinot Blanc.

Opposite: Dr Bob McRitchie, winemaker at Sokol Blosser Winery, sets up a filter in the cellars.

# CHAPTER FIVE
## New York State

ERIE-
CHAUTAUQUA
REGION

FINGER LAKES
REGION

HUDSON
RIVER
REGION

NEW YORK
CITY AND
LONG ISLAND

After California New York State is by far the largest wine-producing area with over 40,000 acres of vineyards and containing the oldest operating winery at Washingtonville in the Hudson River Valley. The state has three main producing areas, the largest being the Finger Lakes Region; perhaps enthusiastic wine producers may be excused for calling it the Finger-licking Lakes Region. The region takes its name from the long lakes in the north Appalachian Plain which on the map look like the extended fingers of a hand. They lie just south of Lake Ontario and to the east of Erie and the Niagara Falls. The other regions are that of Erie-Chautauqua alongside the shore of Lake Erie between Erie and Niagara; and the Hudson River Valley Region, one of the nation's oldest wine-producing areas, just north of New York City. There are a few wineries on Long Island but only one grows its own grapes there.

The Finger Lakes are glacial in origin, long and deep with steep sides. Best known in the context of wine are Lakes Canandaigua and Keuka, the latter being an Indian word for crooked, Lake Keuka being shaped like the letter Y. Largest are Lakes Seneca and Cayuga. The scenery is little short of magnificent with rolling hills covered by trees, vineyards and farmlands setting off the rich blue of the lakes. The region's principal virtues from the vinegrowing point of view are its soil and climate. At the foot of Lake Keuka is Hammondsport, the center of the wine industry. Early settlers in the area at the beginning of the 19th century were struck by the similarity of the land to that of the Rhine Valley of Germany. The stony, well-drained slopes are well suited to the growing of grapes and the lakes themselves serve to temper the extreme cold of the winters, reducing the danger of frost damage by slowing up spring growth and conversely helping to keep the vines warm during treacherous autumn nights. The first experiments in vinegrowing here could flippantly be called

Previous page: Winter snows do not stop the chore of pruning grapevines in the Finger Lakes. Millions of vines are pruned each winter

Catawba grapes, the native North American variety, whose wine was described by Longfellow as having 'a taste more divine, more dulcet, delicious and dreamy.'

Casks in the Aging Cellar of the Brotherhood Winery.

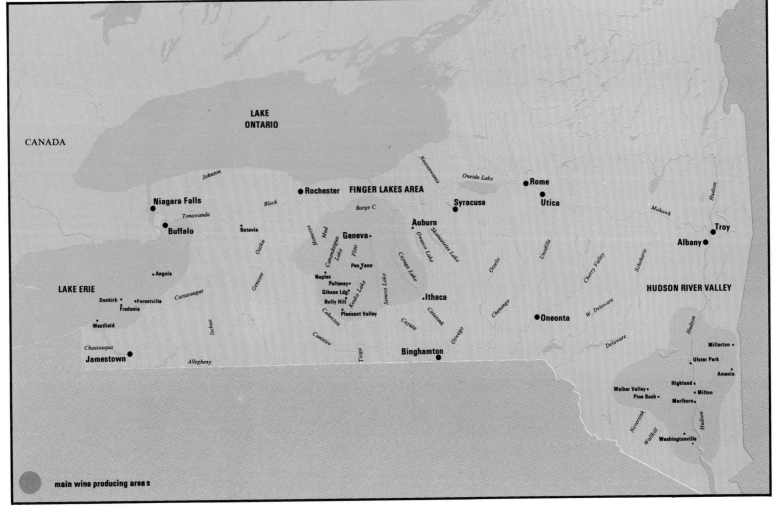

CANADA

LAKE ONTARIO

*Johnson*

● Rochester FINGER LAKES AREA ● Rome

Niagara Falls *Black* ● Syracuse ● Utica

*Tonawanda* *Barge C* *Mohawk*

● Buffalo ● Batavia Geneva ● Auburn Troy ●

*Oatka* *Mud* *Honeoye Lake* *Canandaigua Lake* *Flint* *Pen Yann* *Owasco Lake* *Skaneateles Lake* *Cayuga Lake* *Otselic* *Unadilla* Albany ●

● Angola *Genesee* Naples *Cherry Valley* *Schoharie* HUDSON RIVER VALLEY

LAKE ERIE *Cattaraugus* Pultney ● Gibson Ldg ● *Keuka Lake* *Seneca Lake* *Chenango* *W. Delaware*

Dunkirk ● ● Forestville Bully Hill ● Ithaca ● ● Oneonta *Hudson*

● Fredonia *Ischua* Cohocton ● Pleasant Valley *Cayuta* *Catatonk* Millerton ●

● Westfield *Canisteo* *Tioga* *Owego* *Delaware* Ulster Park ●

*Chautauqua* Binghamton ● Amenia ●

Jamestown ● *Allegheny* Highland ● Walker Valley ● ● Milton

Pine Bush ● Marlboro ●

*Hudson*

*Neversink* *Wallkill* Washingtonville ●

● main wine producing areas

Above: Konstantin Frank of Vinifera Cellars in Hammondsport, at his grafting table. Frank is largely responsible for the revolution in eastern winemaking with his vinifera experiments in the 1950s and '60s.

Right: Mechanical harvesting at the century old Widmer Vineyard.

a grave undertaking for they were carried out by the Rector of the Hammondsport Episcopal Church, the Reverend William Bostwick, who made a vineyard not only out of his lawn but out of the churchyard too. Soon his neighbors followed his example and by 1860 the first bonded winery in the United States was opened.

The local grapes in those early days were of the *vitis labrusca* family and for long the wines of the Finger Lake region were noteworthy for their 'foxiness.' In recent years great changes have been made with the introduction of hybrid grapes. It was soon found that white sparkling wines were inclined to be less foxy so they tended to become the traditional product and a large proportion of the wine produced is New York State Champagne, most of it sweet but with good dry varieties for more sophisticated tastes. As in California most of the Finger Lake wineries were set up by emigrés from Europe, who included several of the greatest names in North American wine production. Outstanding among these was Charles Fournier, once winemaker for the famous French Champagne concern Veuve Clicquot, of what is now the Gold Seal Vineyards at Hammondsport. More recently Dr Konstantin Frank, a Russian-born German, who worked for Fournier at Gold Seal and now has his own winery, Vinifera Wine Cellars at Hammondsport, revolutionized the growing of European *vinifera* grapes. This had been thought to be almost impossible in the comparatively cold climate of the Finger Lakes district. Nevertheless several of the big Finger Lake wineries make some of their wines from grapes grown in their own vineyards in California. These include Taylors, also at Hammondsport, said to be one of the largest producers of bottle-fermented sparkling wines in the world; Gold Seal; and Widmer's Wine Cellars at Naples, south of Lake Canandaigua, which has 500 acres of vineyards in the Sonoma Valley.

The Hudson River Valley Region lies close to New York City in the valley of the River Hudson. To the west are the Appalachian Mountains, to the east the Catskills. Until Prohibition it was more important as a wine-producing area than it has been in recent years, in fact only two wine producers of significance survived that era. But today there are distinct signs of a renewal of activity and interest in the area. Out of the dozen or so wineries in the region two were only started in the 1960s and six since 1970. The two that survived Prohibition were the Brotherhood Winery at Washingtonville and the Hudson Valley Wine Company Inc, in Highland. Apart from its own vineyards in the region the Brotherhood uses grapes from the Finger Lake and Erie-Chautauqua region. The Hudson Valley Wine Company Inc which produces estate-bottled wines in its 325-acre vineyard was the private estate of a wealthy Manhattan banking family until 1970.

The native North American grape Cayuga, named after one of the five Finger Lakes.

The Hudson River is over 300 miles long and has been called 'the Rhine of America.' The region of the wineries lies roughly 60 miles south of the state capital, Albany, between New York and Poughkeepsie near the famous military academy, West Point, and the well-known women's college, Vassar. Here the river is particularly beautiful and just south are the famous Palisades, the tall cliffs of basaltic rock which run down in columns to the river and are the delight of tourists from New York City and elsewhere. At Marlboro, just south of Poughkeepsie, is a rather special winery, that of the Benmarl Wine Company which for many years has been a private experimental station with enological and viticultural research sponsored by the Societé des Vignerons. It is the society's members, by the way, who have the privilege of consuming the bulk of the best wines produced. Another rather special winery in the region, only recently started, is in North Salem in Westchester County, almost in New York City itself. Here on a 13-acre vineyard on his 260-acre dairy farm a Manhattan doctor in 1980 produced his first commercial wine, a Seyval Blanc of which he bottled 275 cases, and from an additional five acres he made 130 cases of Maréchal Foch, a deeply colored red. The operation is typical of the resurgence of wine production with hybrid grapes in North America.

120

Picking and packing grapes for transport to a winery.

The quality of soil for growing grapes is not high by strictly agricultural standards. Gravel and stones are as important as loam; the vineyards of Châteauneuf-du-Pape in the Rhône Valley of France, for example look like pebble beaches. It is interesting to be reminded of this by the addresses of some of the Hudson Valley wineries. We find that the winery in North Salem is on Hardscrabble Road, one in Pine Bush is on Brimstone Hill Road and one in Amenia on Flint Hill Road.

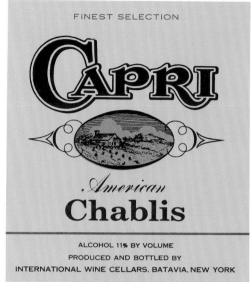

FINEST SELECTION

# CAPRI

*American*

# Chablis

ALCOHOL 11% BY VOLUME
PRODUCED AND BOTTLED BY
INTERNATIONAL WINE CELLARS, BATAVIA, NEW YORK

The Erie-Chautauqua Region lies some 125 miles to the east of Lake Keuka and as its name indicates on the southeastern shore of Lake Erie, running from below Buffalo to the northeastern corner of Pennsylvania. The region may also be said to include the Niagara area to the north between Buffalo and Lake Ontario. The well-drained soil, gravel and shale, of the strip bordering Lake Erie is well suited to growing grapes and as with the Finger Lakes the proximity of the great inland stretch of water helps moderate the effects of the local climate. The center of this region is Fredonia which has two claims to fame — it claims to have had the first gas street lights in the world, and, ironically for the center of a wine-producing area, one of the first units of the Women's Christian Temperance Union was organized there. Over half the vineyards of New York State are situated in this region. Local grapes include Concord, Catawba, Delaware and Niagara but here, also, much has been done with the development of European hybrids. Much of the Concord production goes into grape juice and sweet, heavy wines.

A breakdown of the figures for New York State for 1981 reveals an interesting picture. Unlike California the traditional North American grapes used in winemaking greatly outnumber the French hybrids and other varieties. Of the 69,124 tons of grapes used, 54,760 tons were traditional American and of these 41,000 tons were grown in New York State.

The Niagara grape, another native North American variety, which takes its name from the Niagara Peninsula. It was produced from a cross between Concord and Cassidy grapes in 1868.

## American varieties

| New York State | | From other States and Canada | Used to make wine |
|---|---|---|---|
| Catawba | 9,450 tons | 581 tons | 9,734 tons |
| Concord | 85,481 | 12,714 | 27,382 |
| Delaware | 5,836 | 71 | 5,907 |
| Dutchess | 429 | | 429 |
| Elvira | 3,093 | | 3,093 |
| Ives | 1,162 | | 1,162 |
| Niagara | 7,034 | 442 | 7,053 |
| *French Hybrids* | | | |
| Aurora | 6,682 | | 6,682 |
| Baco Noir | 974 | | 974 |
| de Chaunac | 2,456 | | 2,456 |
| Maréchal Foch | 420 | | 420 |
| Rougeon | 599 | | 599 |
| Seyval Blanc | 403 | | 403 |
| Vitis Vinifera | 319 | | 319 |
| Others | 2,670 | | 2,670 |

**ERIE-CHAUTAUQUA REGION**

**Chadwick Bay Wine Company,** 10001 Route 60, Fredonia, NY.
A new winery started only in 1980 by Rick Mazza and George Borzillert Jr.

**Johnson Estate Wines,** Frederick S Johnson Vineyards, PO Box 52,
West Main Road, Route 20, Westfield, NY 14787.
Rightly called estate wines, because the winery stands in the vineyards, those produced are Aurora Blanc, Seyval Blanc, Delaware, Liebestroepfchen (a semisweet white), Cascade Rosé, Ives Noir and Chancellor Noir.

**Merritt Estate Wines,** King Road, Forestville, NY.
Founded in 1976 by an old-established grape-growing family the winery produces varietal and blended wines including Chautauqua Niagara, Chautauqua Rosé, white and red, Aurora (white), Seyval Blanc, Maréchal Foch, Rosé de Chaunac, Sheridan White and Red.

**Niagara Wine Cellars,** 4100 Route 104, Cambria, NY.
Another newcomer to the New York wine scene this winery was opened only in 1979. It is operated by Paul Lops who has been in the business for over 20 years. Despite its youth it is producing Johannisberg Riesling, Pinot Chardonnay, Siegfried Riesling, Maréchal Foch, Chancellor Nouveau, Vidal Blanc and Leon Millot (a red wine produced under Lilliput label). From native American grapes there are Dutchess Rhine, Dutchess Sauterne and Steuben Rosé.

**Woodbury Vineyards,** South Roberts Road, Dunkirk, NY.
Situated three miles from the shore of Lake Erie this is a small premium winery that is very much a family affair. The present owners' grandparents bought the land in 1910 and developed the vineyard, selling the grapes locally and later further afield. In 1967 Gary F Woodbury, his brother Robert and the latter's wife Page took over and soon planted *vinifera* grapes which now yield Chardonnay, Johannisberg Riesling, Gewürztraminer, Cabernet Sauvignon, and Pinot Gris. The winery, under winemaker Andrew Dabrowski, still produces native American wines from Niagara and Dutchess grapes and from Franco-American hybrids Seyval Blanc, Aurora Blanc and Maréchal Foch. The vineyard also produces Champagnes made by the *méthode Champenoise* as well as other sparkling wines.

**The Barry Wine Company Inc,** 7107 Vineyard Road, Conesus-on-Hemlock Lake, NY 14435.

This winery was started in 1872 by the first Roman Catholic Bishop of Rochester to make sacramental wine. With its 1,000 acres of surrounding vineyard, it was later bought by a Catholic Missionary order and then, in 1968, was taken over by Skip and Ted Cribart who are fourth-generation winemakers. Their wines include Chablis, Rhine, Niagara, Mellow Burgundy, Rosé, Pink Delaware, Pink Catawba, Missouri Riesling, White Delaware, Rosé of Iona, Cream Sherry and Port.

**Bully Hill Vineyard Inc,** Bully Hill Road, RD2, Hammondsport, NY 14840.

Just over a decade old this winery is owned by Walter S Taylor and thereby hangs quite a tale. For Walter S Taylor is the grandson of the founder of the Taylor Wine Company and the Bully Hill Vineyard stands on the original property. But the Taylor Wine Company, the largest producer of premium wines and Champagnes in the eastern United States is now owned by the Coca-Cola Company and it resolutely opposes the public use of the name Taylor in connection with Bully Hill Vineyard and, in fact, obtained court orders preventing it. Walter S who is a versatile man and by no means weak-spirited has had to accept this but has derived some advantageous publicity out of it all. First of all obediently, but very ostentatiously, he blacked out the name Taylor on his labels so that the signature read Walter S, Owner of the Bully Hill Estate — the Taylor surname being still clearly visible under the blacking out. The labels also carried the words 'not connected with, or a successor to, the Taylor

(blacked out) Wine Co.' But perhaps the most forthright riposte was the label shown here for his Billy Goat white wine, attributed to Walter St Bully, Patron of the Estate, and bearing the words 'They have my heritage but they didn't get my goat.' It should be mentioned that versatile Walter designs his own labels. Despite the slight circus atmosphere thus associated with Bully Hill Vineyard (after all Walter S Taylor had an ancestor named Phineas Taylor Barnum) wine production, as might be expected, is a serious matter. Its Champagne, made from Seyval Blanc grapes, is made by the *méthode Champenoise* and its estate-bottled wines include a Baco Noir, Seyval Blanc and Aurora Blanc and a Red, White and Rosé. It also produces regional Vintage wines with the same names. The bottles are sealed with Portuguese corks.

**Canandaigua Wine Company Inc,** 116 Buffalo St, Canandaigua, NY 14424.
This winery is known for a number of brands, particularly Virginia Dare of which it produces a white, a red and a pink. Other brands are Wild Irish Rose, Mother Vineyard and J Roget's Sparkling Wines.

**Casa Larga Vineyards,** 2287 Turk Hill Road, Fairport, NY.
One of the newest of the New York wineries Casa Larga began in the mid-1970s and its wines are just coming on the market. Fairport lies a few miles from Rochester and the waters of Lake Ontario and it was here that Andrew Colaruotolo, a builder of Italian origin, acquired a 98-acre site of which 40 to 45 acres will eventually be a vineyard. The winery is named after the home of Andrew's grandmother in Italy where the family grew grapes and made wine and where he worked as a young man. Andrew is helped by his son John. To begin with they planted a vineyard with native Delaware and Concord grapes but these have now been replaced by French and other hybrids and the wines being produced are: Gewürztraminer, Johannisberg Riesling, Aurora, Pinot Chardonnay, Delaware; in reds: Pinot Noir, Cabernet Sauvignon, De Chaunac, a dry red from French and American hybrids, a red table wine and a Rosé.

1979

*Diamond*

**NEW YORK STATE**
**Alcohol 11.5% by Volume**

HOSMER VINEYARDS

*300 Cases Produced and Bottled by* CHATEAU ESPERANZA
Bluff Point, NY 14417 — Bonded Winery #663

1980

*Aurora Blanc*

NEW YORK STATE
Alcohol 10% by Volume

SMITH VINEYARDS

*500 Cases Produced and Bottled by*
CHATEAU ESPERANZA, Bluff Point, NY 14417
Bonded Winery #663

**Chateau Esperanza,** Route 54A, Box 76, Bluff Point, NY 14417.
One of the youngest of the New York State wineries it is housed in a Greek revival stone mansion built in 1838 with many of the attributes of a French château, particularly its magnificent view over the western arm of Keuka Lake at Bluff Point. Its own vineyards are small but it produces a number of premium varietals from other vineyards and although they have been on the market for only a short time several of the wines have won prizes at the New York State Fair and other eastern wine competitions. The wines are aged in small 50–60 gallon vats and include: a Johannisberg Riesling, Sauvignon Blanc, Cayuga White, Aurora Blanc, Diamond from a native American grape, Seyval Blanc and a rich dessert wine, Ravat.

**Demay Wine Cellars,** Pleasant Valley Road, Hammondsport, NY 14840.
It is run by Serge DeMay, his wife and three children, who came over in 1974 from Vouvray in the Loire Valley in France. Serge comes from a long line of winemakers and is himself a graduate of the Ecole de Viticulture de Beaune. He is already producing a Vin Rosé, Landot, a full-bodied dry red wine, Baco Noir, Chablis Blanc, Delaware and Niagara.

**Four Chimneys Farm Winery,** DD No 1 Hall Road, Himrod, NY 14842.
Started only in 1980 by Walter Pederson, former teacher/editor/farmer it produces Johannisberg Riesling, Chardonnay, Chenin Blanc, Pinot Noir, Cabernet Sauvignon; and from native American grapes Delaware, Dutchess, Cascade, Concord, Elmira. No sprays, herbicides or artificial fertilizers are used.

**Glenora Wine Cellars,** Glenora-on-Seneca, Dundee, NY 14837.
The winery with a capacity of 25,000 gallons concentrates on small quantities of premium wines producing from native American grapes a White Delaware, and from Franco-American hybrids Aurora, Baco Noir Rosé, Cayuga, Seyval Blanc, Maréchal Foch, De Chaunac and Ravat, a white wine, and what it calls Old World Wines — Johannisberg Riesling and Chardonnay.

Pruning on the Gold Seal Vineyards.

**Gold Seal Vineyards Inc,** Hammondsport, NY 14840.
One of the oldest and best known of the Finger Lakes wineries it is situated on the western shores of Keuka Lake and began life as the Urbana Wine Company in 1865 with vineyards extending for 225 acres. The winery was built into the hillside with stone vaults which are used today and by 1875 it had produced 120,000 bottles of what it called Imperial Champagne, later called Gold Seal, and 50,000 bottles of still wine. It survived, only just, the Prohibition years having been given a license to make sacramental wines. From its very beginnings the winery's policy had been to employ

# GOLD SEAL
## American
## Dry Sauterne

MADE AND BOTTLED AT THE WINERY
BY GOLD SEAL VINEYARDS
HAMMONDSPORT, NEW YORK
ALCOHOL 12% BY VOLUME

*Charles Fournier*

ESTATE BOTTLED

## GOLD SEAL VINEYARDS
## Gewürztraminer

NEW YORK STATE WHITE WINE

Produced and bottled at the Winery
by Gold Seal Vineyards
Hammondsport, New York
Alcohol 11.9% by Volume

*Charles Fournier*

Setting up the press at Gold Seal.

European experts to make its wine and one of the outstanding figures in North American wine history, a Frenchman, Charles Fournier, was engaged as winemaker in 1934 after the repeal of Prohibition. He was indeed an expert having been chief winemaker in the famous French Champagne house of Veuve Clicquot in Rheims, France. Gold Seal Vineyards as they later became known achieved further distinction by becoming the first winery to introduce *vinifera* grapes into the Finger Lake district in the 1960s. This was under Dr Konstantin Frank who now has his own winery, Vinifera Wine Cellars (p 134) at Hammondsport. Gold Seal is known for its sparkling wines – Charles Fournier Blanc de Blancs (very dry), Gold Seal Brut Champagne, Gold Seal Extra Dry Champagne, Gold Seal Sparkling Burgundy, Gold Seal Cold Duck (Burgundy and Champagne). In white dinner wines it has Charles Fournier Chablis Nature, Rhine White and Catawba White and in rosés Charles Fournier Rosé Nature and Catawba Pink. Its red table wines include Charles Fournier Burgundy Nature, Catawba Red and Henri Marchant Labrusca Red. It also produces a Gold Seal Cream Sherry, a rich, sweet dessert wine. Gold Seal is now owned by the Seagram Company Ltd.

**Great Western Winery/Pleasant Valley Wine Company,** Hammondsport, NY 14840. This winery, like Taylor's now owned by the Coca-Cola Company, is the oldest in the Finger Lakes region having been started in 1861. For over a century it has been famous for its Great Western Champagne so called because in 1871 a wine authority declared it to be the Great Champagne of the Western World. That there was basis for the claim is shown by the fact that it won an award in Paris in 1867 and in 1910 won the Diploma of Honor, the highest award, in Brussels. Production is by no means limited to Champagne. Great Western is one of the few American wineries that uses the solera system for aging sherries and port. As well as Champagne it produces Sparkling Burgundy, Diamond Chablis, Delaware Moselle, Aurora Sauterne, Seyval Blanc, Baco Noir Burgundy, De Chaunac and Isabella Rosé.

**Hammondsport Wine Company Inc,** 89 Lake St, Hammondsport, NY 14840. This winery has been making wines for over a century, particularly Champagne by the *méthode Champenoise*. It produces only premium wines – Hammondsport Aurora Chablis, Hammondsport Baco Noir as well as Hammondsport New York State Première Cuvée.

**Heron Hill Vineyards,** Hammondsport, NY 14840.
Started in 1968 by Peter Johnstone, an advertising copywriter, and his partner John Ingale Jr, a Neapolitan grapegrower, this winery confines itself to growing only white grapes. It produces Johannisberg Riesling, Chardonnay, Seyval Blanc, Aurora, Rosé, Cayuga and Dutchess.

**Northlake Vineyards,** Cayuga Lake Road, Route 89, Box 271, Romulus, NY 14541.
Fred O'Williams, former engineering manager for IBM, now owner and winemaker of Northlake Vineyards uses his 30-odd acres of vineyard to make only 1,000 gallons of wine at a time, preferring, he says, to be a low-volume, high-quality producer. Wines produced, all estate-bottled, are Baco Noir, Pinot Noir, Riesling, Chardonnay and Cabernet Sauvignon.

**Plane's Cayuga Vineyards,** RD 2 Route 89, Ovid, NY 14521.
Mr and Mrs Robert Plane – he is President of Clarkson College of Technology – have been growing grapes in their vineyard on the eastern side of Lake Seneca since 1972 and their vineyard is one of the largest suppliers of Cayuga grapes in the State. Wine production itself did not start until 1980 and Robert, who is winemaker, produces Chardonnay, Chancellor and De Chaunac.

**The Taylor Wine Company,** County Route 88, Hammondsport, NY 14840.
This is perhaps the most prestigious and best-known of the Eastern United States wineries. It is just over 100 years since it started with a seven-acre vineyard. Today, owned by the Coca-Cola Company, it is the largest producer of premium wines in the

The Great Western Winery, oldest in the Finger Lakes region, renowned for its Champagne.

Right: A mechanical harvester gathering grapes in the vineyard of the Taylor Wine Company at Hammondsport. Fiberglass paddles on the harvester shake the grapes onto a conveyor belt, which feeds into a plastic-lined tote bin.

Below: Modern steel storage cylinders at the Taylor Wine Company.

eastern part of the country and, indeed, is one of the largest producers of bottle-fermented sparkling wines in the world. Some of its best-known wines are labeled Lake County. It makes sherries, port and vermouth and altogether produces 23 premium wines. The winery, architecturally a mixture of ancient and modern, attracts over 100,000 visitors a year. Its products under New York State label include Extra Dry and Brut Champagne, Cream and Golden Sherry, Port, Lake County White, Pink, Red and Gold (a medium, white, semisweet wine). The Lake County wines are all from Franco-American hybrids. Also Rhine, Sauterne, Pink Catawba, Rosé and Burgundy.

More traditional aging in barrels at the Taylor Wine Company.

**Villa D'Ingianni Winery Inc,** 1183 East Lake Rd, Highway 54, Dundee, NY 14837. This winery, owned by Mr and Mrs James Kilgore, with Dr D'Ingianni as winemaker, was opened in 1972 and produces three grades of wine — Premium, varietal and commercial. The premium wines are under a Villa D'Ingianni label and comprise VDI Pinot Chardonnay, Riesling, Ottonel, Delaware, Baco Noir, Isabella (a rosé). Varietals, under a Villa label are Villa Niagara, Rhine, Chablis, Burgundy, Rosé and Pink Catawba.

**Vinifera Wine Cellars Ltd,** RD 2, Hammondsport, NY 14840.
One of the best-known names in the North American wine world is that of Dr Konstantin Frank who some quarter of a century ago — he was then with Gold Seal Vineyards — took the lead in growing *vinifera* grapes in New York State — an achievement then thought impossible. He now owns and runs Vinifera, whose vineyards lie above Keuka Lake and where he grows 60 varieties of top-grade European wine grapes including Fetjaska, a Hungarian grape from which Russia's best Champagne is made, and Sereksia Tschornay from which the Ukraine's best pink wine comes. His wines include Johannisberg Riesling Nature Late Harvest, Pinot Chardonnay, Gewürztraminer, Pinot Noir, Cabernet Sauvignon, Gamay Beaujolais, Sereksia (rosé), Saperavi, Rkatziteli, Pinot Gris. He also makes Port, Sherry (Pedro Chimines) and Furmint Tokay.

**Wagner Vineyards,** Lodi, NY 14860.
Very much a family affair run by owner Bill Wagner, his two sons and a daughter this winery produces only estate produced and bottled wines. They include Aurora, Seyval Blanc, Wagner's Seyval, Delaware, De Chaunac, Rosé, Alta B (a medium-bodied red), Wagner's Red, Chardonnay, Riesling and Rougeon (a light-bodied red).

**Widmer Wine Cellars Inc**, Naples, NY 14512.

Almost exactly a century ago (in 1882) John Jacob Widmer, a Swiss, bought and cleared a plot of hillside woodland near Naples at the foot of Lake Canandaigua, planted it with vines and created a wine business which has grown into one of the top five in the Finger Lake district. It produces over 35 different types of wine, noteworthy among them Lake Niagara (a white, semidry varietal), Haut Sauterne, Sauterne, Rhine, Cayuga White, Foch, Lake Roselle (rosé), Cream and Dry Sherry, Port, Crackling Lake Niagara and Lake Niagara Light.

The modern complex of buildings now housing the Widmer Wine Cellars Inc, a winery started a century ago.

Delivering grapes for crushing at the Widmer Wine Cellars in Naples, NY.

**Hermann J Wiemer Vineyard,** Box 4, Route 14, Dundee, NY 14837.
It is early days for this winery established only in 1979 by Hermann J Wiemer who had his wine education in Germany and started experimenting in grape growing and grafting in 1971. The vineyard concentrates on Johannisberg Riesling, Chardonnay, Pinot Noir and Gewürztraminer and produced its first wines — Johannisberg Riesling and Pinot Chardonnay in 1979.

Mechanical harvesting in the Widmer vineyard.

## HUDSON RIVER REGION

**Benmarl Wine Company,** Marlboro, NY 12542.
This small but exclusive winery serves two purposes. It is a private experimental station providing enological and viticultural data aimed at helping the reborn wine industry of the Hudson River region and it supplies most of its wines, especially the finest, to the members of the Societé des Vignerons who are its sponsors. Under the Cuvée des Vignerons label it produces a Chardonnay, a Johannisberg Riesling and a Mousseux. Other labels include Marlboro Village Seyval Blanc, Marlboro Village Red and White, Hudson Region Red and White, Mountain Range Seyval Blanc and Chancellor.

**Brimstone Hill Vineyard,** Brimstone Hill Rd, RD 2, Box 142, Pine Bush, NY 12566.
Only 80 miles northwest of New York City, in the foothills of the Shawangunk Mountains on the west bank of the Hudson River this is a small winery and Richard and Valerie Eldridge who run it intend that it should remain so. Production for the foreseeable future is expected to remain under 5,000 gallons. Started in 1969 it produces Brimstone Hill Red (from a blend of Baco Noir, Maréchal Foch and Chambourçin); Brimstone Hill White (from Aurora, Seyval Blanc and Rayon d'Or) and Brimstone Hill Rosé (from Chelois, SV5247 and Cascade).

**Brotherhood Winery,** 35 North Street, Washingtonville, NY 10992.
If for no other reason this winery would deserve special mention for it is the oldest operating winery in the United States, its vineyards at Washingtonville in the Hudson River Valley having been laid out in 1810 and its first wine produced in 1839. Its founder, a Frenchman named Jean-Jacques, an elder of the Presbyterian Church, made sacramental wine. On the other side of the river was a religious

Below right: Sizeable storage vats in the cellars of the Brotherhood Winery, Washingtonville, founded in 1810 by a Frenchman who was an elder of the Presbyterian Church.

Below: The stone building of the Brotherhood Winery, which despite its name is now owned and run by a woman.

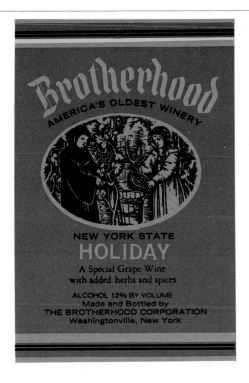

**Brotherhood**
AMERICA'S OLDEST WINERY

NEW YORK STATE
HOLIDAY

A Special Grape Wine
with added herbs and spices

ALCOHOL 12% BY VOLUME
Made and Bottled by
THE BROTHERHOOD CORPORATION
Washingtonville, New York

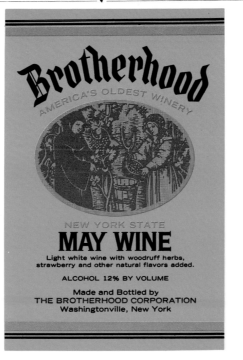

**Brotherhood**
AMERICA'S OLDEST WINERY

NEW YORK STATE
MAY WINE

Light white wine with woodruff herbs,
strawberry and other natural flavors added.

ALCOHOL 12% BY VOLUME
Made and Bottled by
THE BROTHERHOOD CORPORATION
Washingtonville, New York

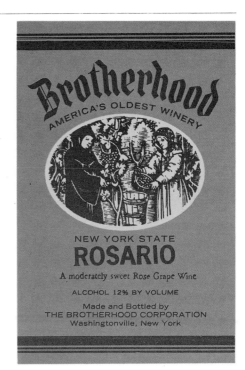

**Brotherhood**
AMERICA'S OLDEST WINERY

NEW YORK STATE
ROSARIO

A moderately sweet Rose Grape Wine

ALCOHOL 12% BY VOLUME
Made and Bottled by
THE BROTHERHOOD CORPORATION
Washingtonville, New York

community known as The Brotherhood which also sold wine. It moved to the West and in 1896 its Hudson Valley winery was taken over by the then owner of Jacques winery who retained the name Brotherhood for the combined operation. Although it still makes sacramental wines it is now an entirely commercial operation. It has an additional claim to special mention for since 1974, despite its name, it has been owned and run by one of North America's first women winemakers, Mrs E Farrell and her daughter Anne. It gets its grapes from its own vineyards in the Hudson River Valley and in Penn Yan in the Finger Lake area as well as from growers from Lake Erie to the Hudson. Its products include St Vincent Burgundy, dry and full-bodied; Jubilee Red, semidry; Harvest Blush Rosé; Jubilee Chablis, white and dry; Vinecrest Sauterne, fruity and mellow; Rhineling, medium dry. What are called Special Wines include: May Wine, a light white with woodruff herbs, strawberry and other flavors; Holiday, a spicy red often served hot; Golden Delaware, a sweet white wine. Dutchess, a dry white wine and Catawba, a semisweet pink are made with native North American grapes of the same names. The winery also makes ports and sherries.

**Cagnasso Winery,** Marlboro, NY 12542.
A recent newcomer to the scene, this is a small farm winery whose first vintage was in 1977. All its wines are aged in wood and bottled in 50 gallon lots. It produces Bianco Classico (a classic dry white), Moselle, Chianti, Rosso Amabile (dry red), Vino Rosé, White Favorite, Labrusca (sweet dark red), Leon Millot, De Chaunac, Seyval Blanc.

**Cascade Mountain Vineyards,** Flint Hill Rd, Amenia, NY 12501.
Not many wineries can claim to have started as a special studies project for high school. This one did, in 1977, for Charles, son of novelist Bill Wetmore. Father decided to continue and expand the operation to make quality wines and the winery already produces in modest quantities a Harvest Red, White, Rosé and Reserved Red. It also produces two 'everyday' wines called 'Le Hamburger Red' and 'A Little White Wine.' The Harvest wines are bottled and sold within a year of harvest, the Reserved Red aged in barrels for a year and then in bottle.

**El Paso Winery,** Route 9 W, Box 170, Ulster Park, NY 12487.
This winery located in a reconstructed farm building, was started in 1968 by Publio
Felipe Beltra, now a US citizen, who had worked in his father's winery in Uruguay.
El Paso wines — the first was sold in 1979 — are made from Franco-American hybrid
grapes and include Vino de Mesa (a dry red), Rosado (semidry), Blanco (a semidry
white), Mellow Red (sweet dessert), Hudson Valley Gold (sweet dessert) and Claret.

**Hudson Valley Wine Company Inc,** Blue Point Rd, Highland, NY 12528.
Until 1970 this winery with its 325-acre vineyard was the strictly private concern
of a wealthy Manhattan banking family (the Bolognesis) and was noteworthy for its

The interior of storage vats need to be
inspected from time to time. Here the
inspector crawls out of one of the vats at the
Hudson Valley Wine Company Inc.

Above: In this building at the Hudson Valley Wine Company, visitors can see the complete process of winemaking.

Right: This is how grapes were pressed in Europe – and in some places still are. At the Hudson Valley Winery, visitors can watch – or even participate in – an annual Grape Stomping Championship.

**HUDSON VALLEY
CHELOIS**

*A dry red New York State varietal wine
with the distinctive character of the Chelois grape,
a superior European-American hybrid.
Alcohol 12% by volume.*

MADE, BLENDED & BOTTLED BY THE
HUDSON VALLEY WINE CO., HIGHLAND, N.Y.

**HUDSON VALLEY
DELAWARE**

*A dry white New York State varietal wine
with the distinctive character of the Delaware grape,
an early hybrid of mysterious origin.
Alcohol 12% by volume.*

MADE, BLENDED & BOTTLED BY THE
HUDSON VALLEY WINE CO., HIGHLAND, N.Y.

HUDSON VALLEY WINERY
**Hot Rumour**
Grape wine flavored
with cinnamon & clove.

A mulled wine punch prepared according to the traditional recipe of its namesake. Hot Rumour originated in the inns and road houses of 16th century England. Serve steaming hot in mugs or glasses. Do not boil.
Alcohol 12% by volume.
Produced & Bottled by Hudson Valley Wine Co., Highland, N.Y.

HUDSON VALLEY *Haut Sauterne* New York State

*A classic New York State table wine of unusual fragrance and flavor. Serve well chilled with white meat, poultry and fish. Produced, blended and bottled by Hudson Valley Wine Co., Highland, N.Y. Alcohol 12% by volume.*

HUDSON VALLEY *Burgundy* New York State

*A soft, red New York State table wine with a light, fragrant bouquet. Serve slightly chilled with red meats, cheese or barbecue. Made, blended and bottled by Hudson Valley Wine Co., Highland, N.Y. Alcohol 12% by volume.*

HUDSON VALLEY *Rosé* New York State

*A dry, light New York State table wine with exhilarating flavor and bouquet. Serve well chilled—"the one bottle wine cellar." Produced, blended and bottled by Hudson Valley Wine Co., Highland, N.Y. Alcohol 12% by volume.*

The press room at the Hudson Valley Wine Company.

fine premium wines. In that year it was acquired by Herbert Feinberg, whose wine-maker is William Voss, and is now open to the public seven days a week. It continues to produce premium wines including Maréchal Foch, Seyval Blanc, Chelois and Delaware, Burgundy, Claret, Haut Sauterne, Chablis, White Burgundy, Pink Catawba, Rosé, Blanc de Blanc Champagne, Extra dry, Brut and Pink Champagnes, Sparkling Burgundy and Cold Duck.

**North East Vineyard,** Silver Mountain Rd, Millerton, NY 12546.
A real pocket handkerchief vineyard covering only two acres and producing about 300 gallons of Red (75 percent Maréchal Foch, 25 percent Baco Noir) and Aurora White. It is run by George Green, a heart specialist, his wife and sons. It was first planted in 1972.

**North Salem Vineyard,** Hardscrabble Road, North Salem, Westchester County, NY.
You cannot get much nearer to New York City itself than North Salem and you cannot get much smaller or newer than North Salem Vineyard, the winery of Dr George Naumberg, a New York psychiatrist. The vineyard is only 13 acres in extent, produces two wines — a Seyval Blanc (its first production of 275 cases was in the spring of 1981) and a North Salem Vineyard Foch from Maréchal Foch grapes (which yielded 130 cases). Dr Naumberg began by planting the vineyard with a wide variety of grapes and for several years simply sold the grapes and grapejuice to home winemakers, but he then decided to concentrate on the Seyval Blanc and Maréchal Foch aiming eventually to produce 5,000 cases of the former and 4,000 of the latter.

**Royal Wine Corporation/Kedem Winery,** Dock Rd, Milton, NY 12547.
This considerable winery, producer of fine Kosher wines, began its life in Czechoslovakia, then part of the Austro-Hungarian Empire, in 1848. Exactly 100 years later it moved to the United States, to lower Manhattan, and eventually, 10 years later, ended up in the Hudson Valley. It has a production capacity of nearly 1,000,000 gallons of more than 20 different wines including Haut Sauterne, Rosé, Dry and Naturally Sweet Concord, Chablis, Le Blanc de Blanc, De Chaunac, Seyval Blanc, Cream, White and Pink Concord, Dry and Pink Champagne, Cold Duck and Sparkling Burgundy.

**Valley Vineyards,** Oregon Trail Road, Walker Valley, NY 12588.
Another new and small farm winery. Its vineyards at present cover only seven acres but are in the process of expanding to about double that size. Its owner, chairman of

144

Roy Lichtenstein "Yellow Brushstroke II" Collection of the Artist

# Hargrave Vineyard Long Island Chardonnay "Collectors Series" 1981

Estate Grown, Produced & Bottled By Hargrave Vineyard, Cutchogue, N.Y. 13.0% Alcohol By Volume

This bottling consists of 575 cases, 250 magnums and 21 double magnums, offered for sale in New York only.

the physical education department of the local County Community College is Professor Gary Dross. His wines, first sold in 1979, are all estate-bottled and are Aurora, Autumn White, Valley Rosé and Autumn Red.

## NEW YORK CITY AND LONG ISLAND

**Hargrave Vineyards,** Cutchogue, Long Island, NY 11935.
Grapes were grown in Cutchogue as far back as the early 1700s and wines were being produced on Long Island later in the same century. These activities ceased in the 19th century and it was left to Alexander Hargrave and his family to revive them. In 1973 he began planting up this 45-acre vineyard on Great Peconic Bay with *vinifera* grapes and is producing these estate-grown varietals: Pinot Noir, Cabernet Sauvignon, Chardonnay and Sauvignon Blanc.

**Monarch Wine Company Inc,** 4500 Second Avenue, Brooklyn, NY 112322.
A glance at the address and it will be realized that there is not a vineyard in sight from this, one of America's largest wineries with storage capacity for 5,000,000 gallons. In the industrial complex of Brooklyn it looks out on the Manhattan skyscrapers while sterilized glass tank trucks containing the juice of crushed grapes from elsewhere in New York State roll up to the winery doors. Monarch is famous for its Kosher wines sold under the label Manischewitz including dry and pink semidry Champagne made by the *méthode Champenoise*, Sparkling Burgundy, Cold Duck and Spumanti. Its other wines include Pol D'Argent Champagne (dry, pink and semidry), Sparkling Burgundy, Cold Duck and Spumante and St Laurent Champagne and Château Imperial Champagne with the same variations. The winery's equipment is entirely modern and capable of bottling 250,000 bottles daily.

**Schapiro's Wine Company Ltd,** 126 Rivington St, NY, NY 10002.
Situated also far from any vineyards — in fact in downtown Manhattan between the Bowery and Roosevelt Parkway — Schapiro's is another winery specializing in Kosher wines. The grapes used by the winery come from upstate New York and although the winery makes as much as 500,000 gallons annually it limits its sales to 350,000, leaving 150,000 for aging and blending. It offers 26 different wines including: Extra Heavy Concord (the traditional sweet, heavy Passover wine), Medium Dry Concord, Burgundy, Cream White Concord, White, Dry and Pink Champagne, Sparkling Burgundy, Cold Duck, Spumante, Rosé and Chablis.

# CHAPTER SIX
## Other U.S. States

MICHIGAN
MARYLAND
OHIO

SOUTHERN
STATES
VIRGINIA

## MICHIGAN

Previous page: New vines planted on the Boskydel Vineyards overlooking Lake Leelanau.

This midwestern state is bordered in the north by Lake Superior, in the west by Lake Michigan and in the east by Lakes Huron and Erie. The winds that blow across their waters moderate the extreme hot and cold temperatures that are a feature of the Lower Peninsula and this has helped to make the state the fourth largest producer of wine in the United States after California, New York and Washington. Its vineyards which cover 12,500 acres, are concentrated mainly but not entirely in the southwest corner near the town of Kalamazoo. There are a few vineyards and wineries at the northeastern end of Lake Michigan and one or two in the southeast of the state. In the area around Kalamazoo the cold air from Lake Michigan delays the budding of the grapes so that the danger of frost is greatly reduced and the same is the case at the northeastern end of the Lake. Similarly in the fall the Lake helps hold off the frosts thus protecting the ripening grapes. The soil of the main growing area is sandy and gravelly.

There are some 15 wineries in the state – not all of them grow their own grapes – and, again typical of the American wine scene today, only six of them existed before 1970. The oldest and one of the largest actually began in Canada in 1921, then moved to Detroit, Michigan with the repeal of Prohibition and did not move into its present headquarters in Paw Paw until 1937. Many still produce wines from native North American grapes such as Concord but in common with the rest of the country the use of hybrid Franco-American grapes is becoming more widespread. Michigan has one dubious distinction – it claims to have originated the blending of American Champagne and American Burgundy, the sparkling red wine called Cold Duck.

## WINERIES

**Boskydel Vineyards and Winery,** Route 1, Box 522, Lake Leelanau, Mi 49653.
This lies on a sunny slope facing southwest on the shore of Lake Leelanau. It is another small family business, the vineyard extending over only 25 acres. Head of the business is Bernie Rink, a librarian by profession but a wine-producer by descent as it were. His great-grandfather grew grapes along the Moselle River in

A beautiful sight! Grapes under snow at the Boskydel Vineyards.

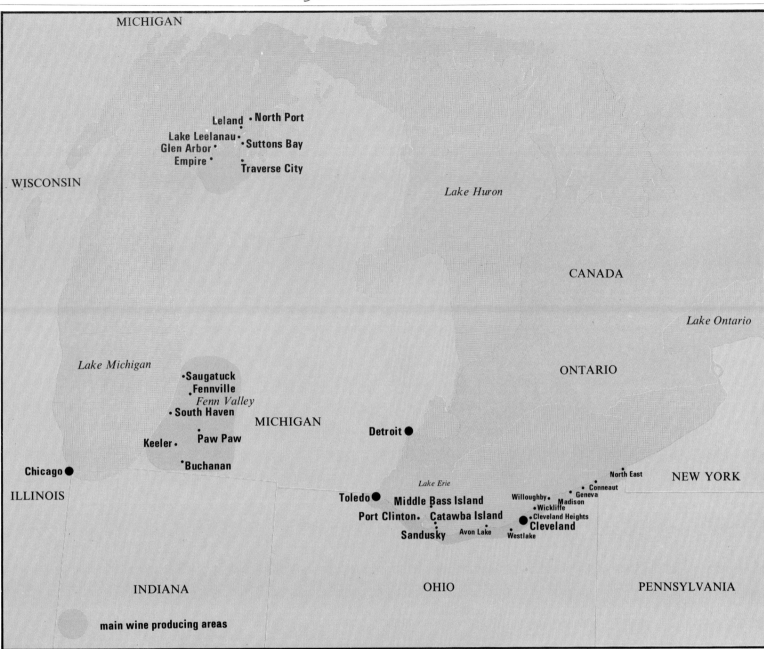

MICHIGAN

Leland • • North Port
Lake Leelanau •
Glen Arbor • • Suttons Bay
Empire • • Traverse City

WISCONSIN

*Lake Huron*

CANADA

*Lake Ontario*

*Lake Michigan*

ONTARIO

• Saugatuck
• Fennville
*Fenn Valley*
• South Haven MICHIGAN
Keeler • • Paw Paw
• Buchanan

Detroit ●

Chicago ●

ILLINOIS

North East •
NEW YORK

*Lake Erie*
• Conneaut
Willoughby • • Geneva
Toledo ● Middle Bass Island • Madison
• Wickliffe
Port Clinton • Catawba Island • Cleveland Heights
Sandusky Avon Lake ● Cleveland
Westlake

INDIANA

OHIO

PENNSYLVANIA

**main wine producing areas**

Chancellor Noir grapes from the Boskydel Vineyard.

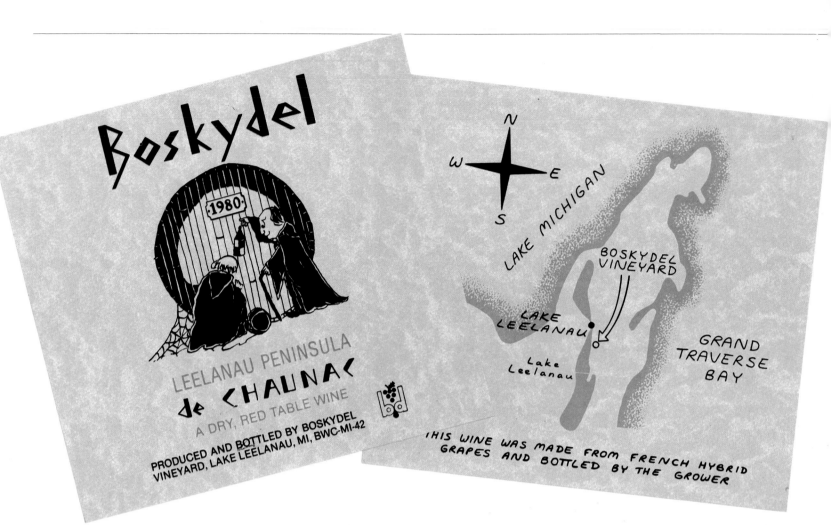

Right: The Boskydel Vineyards and winery experiences a Michigan winter.

Above: Setting up end posts for supporting vines in the Boskydel Vineyard.

Far right: The Boskydel proprietor's son rallies round at harvest time.

Europe, his father and grandfather grew grapes in Ohio and his father, Bernie admits, did a little bootlegging during the Prohibition years. In 1965 he planted 30 varieties of Franco-American hybrid grapes from which he selected six and by 1977 he was beginning to sell wine from the 3,000 gallons he produced that year. He aims to produce 10,000 gallons annually. Present varieties include Johannisberg Riesling, de Chaunac Red and Rosé, Seyval Blanc, and Vignoles, a dry white.

Above: Boskydel is very much a family affair here David Rink carries out tests in the laboratory.

Right: Jim Rink empties grapes into a crusher.

**Bronte Champagne and Wines Company,** 930 West Eight Mill Road, Detroit, Mi.
One of the oldest wineries in Michigan, it has some curious historic links. Its 150-acre vineyard at Keeler in Van Buren County must be the only vineyard in North America that was planted by German prisoners of war (stationed in nearby Hartford in 1943). It was in a house on the property that, ironically, a branch of the Women's Christian Temperance Union was opened in 1879 to 'help stem the issuance of many unnecessary prescriptions,' (for whiskey). Also the wooden storage tanks in the main cellar once belonged to Al Capone, the Chicago gangster, and were acquired when his brewery was closed by the government. The winery was started in Detroit in 1933 on the repeal of Prohibition by a group headed by Dr T W Wozniak, a dentist and father of the present president. It moved to Keeler during World War II and it was there in 1953 that the first Franco-American hybrid grapes were planted in Michigan. These were Baco Noir and were introduced by Angelo Spinazze, a viticulturist and enologist, who is now Vice-President and winemaker. The winery has a storage capacity of 1,000,000 gallons and among its products are: Bronte and Jean Doreau Champagne; Baco Noir, Burgundy, Maréchal Foch among the reds; and Pink Delaware, Rosé, Pink, Catawba, Pink Chablis and Scarlet Rosé. Its white wines include a Rhine wine, Chablis, Aurora Blanc and Vidal Blanc. In dessert wines it makes sweet sherry, port and vermouth and, another historic detail, the winery claims to have devised bottled Cold Duck.

**Château Grand Travers Ltd,** 12239 Center Rd, Traverse City, Mi.
Founded 1974. Owner, O'Keefe Center Ltd; winemaker, Steve Murphy. Has 100 acres of vineyards and storage capacity of 50,000 gallons. Brand names include Château Grand Travers and Grand Traverse Vineyard.

**Fenn Valley Vineyards and Wine Cellar,** 6130 122nd Avenue, Fennville, Mi 49408.
This is a young winery started only in 1973 on 230 acres of farmland of which about 100 are suitable for growing grapes. Just over a half of these are in use and the area is being slowly increased. The vineyards are in the Fenn Valley and the winery in Fennville, which has been formally recognized by the US Treasury as a viticultural area, is a few miles from the shore of Lake Michigan south of Grand Rapids. The winery is a small family business with a storage capacity of 60,000 gallons, the

**Fenn Valley**

MICHIGAN

**REGAL RED**

WINE

A MICHIGAN DRY RED TABLE WINE

*A full-bodied dry, red table wine blend made in the classic European style and carefully aged in small oak casks.*

PRODUCED AND BOTTLED IN OUR NATURALLY COOL CELLARS BY
FENN VALLEY VINEYARDS • FENNVILLE, MICHIGAN 49408
BWC-MI-38          11½% ALCOHOL BY VOLUME

FENN VALLEY WINE IS A LIVING, NATURAL BEVERAGE.

Although carefully clarified before being bottled, tartrate crystals or sediment may develop as the wine continues to mature in the bottle. Such sediments are to be expected and are not a defect in a naturally produced wine.

Please decant or pour carefully for maximum enjoyment.

**Fenn Valley**

FENN VALLEY is dedicated to the production of classic table wines from European style wine grapes which can withstand the severe climate of the Great Lakes Region. At FENN VALLEY, just as in Germany, the best wines come from those grapes which must struggle for survival. Located near Lake Michigan on the sandy hills of Michigan's Lower Peninsula, this small family-owned wine cellar combines the art of the Old-World techniques with modern vinifying technology to produce delightful grape and fruit wines styled after those of western Europe. Fine wines require select fully ripened grapes, skill, time, and patience — they cannot be hurried. All important barrel and bottle aging is done in FENN VALLEY's naturally cool cellars where the maturing wines are carefully protected from flavor loss and deterioration. Visit us and see the pride and care which goes into every bottle of our fine table and fruit wines.

SERVE COLD

**Fenn Valley**

FENNVILLE

*Vidal Blanc Reserve*

1981

ESTATE BOTTLED

A PREMIUM WHITE TABLE WINE

PRODUCED AND BOTTLED IN OUR NATURALLY COOL CELLARS BY
FENN VALLEY VINEYARDS • FENNVILLE, MICHIGAN 49408
BWC-MI-38

FENN VALLEY WINE IS A LIVING, NATURAL BEVERAGE.

Although carefully clarified before being bottled, tartrate crystals or sediment may develop as the wine continues to mature in the bottle. Such sediments are to be expected and are not a defect in a naturally produced wine.

Please decant or pour carefully for maximum enjoyment.

*Vidal Blanc*

FENN VALLEY is dedicated to the production of classic table wines from European style wine grapes which can withstand the severe climate of the Great Lakes Region. The grapes used in this wine were carefully nurtured through the growing season and were picked on 20 October when they were 20.1° Brix. The wine was fermented cool with a select strain of European wine yeast to preserve the delicate fruit of the Vidal grape. The fermentation was stopped when the wine had an alcohol content of 7.9% by volume. The finished wine, which has a total acidity of 1.12% by weight and a natural residual sugar content of 4.2% by weight, was bottled the following March and has captured the fruit and character unique to Vidal grapes grown in the Fennville viticultural area along the shores of Lake Michigan.

winemaker and farm manager being Douglas Welsch. It employs only six people full-time, engaging outside labor for harvesting, pruning etc. Only European *vinifera* grapes are used and already the winery's premium products include an estate-bottled Seyval Blanc, a Johannisberg Riesling, a Vidal Blanc and a Vignoles. Other wines include: a Gewürztraminer, American Chancellor (a very dry red), Regal Red and Regal White and a Blanc de Blanc. Once the vineyard is fully established it should meet all the demands of the winery so that all wine can be estate-bottled.

**Fink Winery,** 208 Main, Dundee, Mi 48131.
Founded 1976. Owner, Carl E Fink. Storage capacity 6,000 gallons, fermenting 6,000 gallons. Brand name Crest.

**Frontenac Vineyards Inc,** 3418 W Michigan Avenue, Paw Paw, Mi 49079.
Founded 1933. Storage capacity 500,000 gallons, fermenting 50,000 gallons. Produces table, dessert and cocktail wines. Brand names are Frontenac, Château Club and Chantilly.

Backed by the blue waters of Lake Michigan is this small and new vineyard the Good Harbor Vineyards.

Inset: Seyval Blanc Grapes.

**Good Harbor Vineyards,** Rt Box 891, Lake Leelanau, Mi 49653.
Tucked up on the northeastern shore of Lake Michigan some 120 miles north of Grand Rapids this is one of the smallest and newest of the state's wineries. At present they have 15 acres of vineyard planted with *vinifera* grapes and aim to limit themselves to 50 acres. Owned and operated by the Simpson family who have been in the fruit-growing but not winemaking business for over 30 years, their wines have still to be tested – their first crush was in 1980. Their production list covers Ravat 51 (Vignoles), Seyval Blanc, Aurora, Riesling and Chardonnay. President of the firm and winemaker is D Bruce Simpson.

**Lakeside Vineyard Inc,** 13581 Red Arrow Highway, Harbert, Mi.
Founded 1975. Owner, Cecil E Pond; winemaker, Art Sandtveit. Has four acres of vineyards. Storage capacity 500,000 gallons. Makes table and dessert wines.

good harbor vineyards

1981 Michigan
**DeChaunac Rose'**
Produced and Bottled by
Good Harbor Vineyards
Lake Leelanau, Michigan 49653
BW-MI-49
Alcohol 11% by Volume

**Leelanau Wine Cellars Ltd,** US 31 So, Traverse City, Mi.
Founded 1975. Winemaker, Edward J Vandyne; enologist, Nathan G Stackhouse Jr.
Has 30 acres of vineyards. Storage and fermentation capacity 85,000 gallons.
Produces table wines including Champagne.

**Milan Wineries,** 4109 Joe St at 6000 Michigan Ave, Detroit, Mi 48210.
Founded 1944. Winemaker, Charles Milan, President and Robert Rubinstein, Vice-
President. Storage capacity 500,000 gallons. Produces table and dessert wines.
Brand names are Cadillac Club and Nature Boy.

**St Julian Wine Company Inc,** 716 S Kalamazoo Str, PO Box 127, Paw Paw,
Mi 49079.
This is one of the largest of the State's wineries and was originally established in
Ontario, Canada, by an Italian named Mariano Meconi in 1921. He moved across to

**St·Julian**

*American*
## PEACH
**Flavored Wine Cocktail**
GRAPE WINE AND NATURAL PEACH FLAVOR

750
ML

# St·Julian

*Michigan*
*Dew*

*American*
## WHITE GRAPE WINE
ALCOHOL 16% BY VOLUME

MADE AND BOTTLED BY
ST. JULIAN WINE CO., INC.
PAW PAW

MADE AND BOTTLED WHERE THE GRAPES GROW

כשר
כשר לפסח

# SHOLOM

**MICHIGAN KOSHER**
## SWEET CONCORD WINE
SWEETENED WITH EXCESS SUGAR
ALCOHOL 12% BY VOLUME

BEST WHEN SERVED COLD

0  88587 09150

כשר תחת השגחת
פרם רב מאיר
SUPERVISED BY

PRODUCED AND
BOTTLED BY
**ST. JULIAN WINE CO., INC.**
PAW PAW
MICH. 49079

## Chateau St. Julian
**MICHIGAN BRUT CHAMPAGNE**

NATURAL FERMENTATION BULK PROCESS (CHARMAT)

*Sparkling Wine*

ALCOHOL 12% BY VOL.

...CED & BOTTLED BY **St. Julian Wine Co.,** PAW PAW, MICHIGAN

**St·Julian**

*Michigan*
## Niagara

Serve
Well
Chilled

This Semi-dry White Wine
captures the truly fresh and fruity
essence of Niagara grapes picked
at the peak of ripeness.

Produced and bottled by St. Julian Wine Co.
Paw Paw, Michigan, 49079 Alcohol 11% by Vol.

0  88587 30750

...n Vin Rose' is a fine
...able wine that owes its
...white wine grapes and
...ste to red wine grapes.
...nified separately and
...r peak to create this
...led.

..., Mariano Meconi
... born in Falaria, Italy.
... the patron saint of
...ted in the heart of the
...istrict. Our winery is
...ublic for tours and
... year around.

*Catherman*
Chas. Catherman,
Winemaker

Winery
Founded 1921

750

**St·Julian**

MICHIGAN
## VIN ROSE'
PREMIUM SEMI-DRY TABLE WINE

ALCOHOL 11% BY VOLUME

PROUDLY PRODUCED AND BOTTLED BY
ST. JULIAN WINE CO. INC.
PAW PAW, VAN BUREN COUNTY
MICHIGAN U.S.A. BONDED WINERY MI-23

157

Detroit, Michigan after the repeal of Prohibition in 1933 and four years later to Paw Paw near the shore of Lake Michigan in the main grape-growing area. The business was then called the Italian Wine Company but recognizing anti-Italian feeling during World War II Meconi changed the name to St Julian Wine Company. The disguise was a thin one for St Julian was the patron saint of his birthplace but the business flourished. Originally the grapes used were native North American such as Concord, Niagara and Delaware but in recent years the winery began buying Franco-American hybrids which now account for 80 percent of its consumption and come from 60 regular growers within a 40-mile radius of Paw Paw. The winery with a 1,500,000 gallons storage capacity is still controlled by the Meconi family with David Braganini, whose father Apollo was the founder's son-in-law, as President. It recently opened a second winery at Frankenmuth near Saginaw where the grapes from a 10-acre contracted local vineyard are to be used initially to produce St Julian Solera Cream Sherry. The winery uses a variety of hybrid grapes including Baco Noir, Foch, Chelois, Vidal Blanc and Seyval Blanc and continues to use the Native Niagara. Charles Catherman, St Julian's winemaker, claims that unlike California grapes those of Michigan are ripe and balanced at a lower natural sugar content which means that they do not have to be picked before the grapes are ripe in order to produce the light, aromatic quality and the lower alcoholic content, which he likes. In 1982 St Julian introduced a Light Chablis with a seven to nine percent alcoholic content. The winery's products include a dry white Rhine, a pink Chablis, Vin Rosé, Sauterne, Burgundy, a Michigan Dew (with 16 percent alcoholic content); a White and Dark Port; Friar's White, Noir and Rosé; Cold Duck and Champagne made by the Charmat bulk process. St Julian are planning also to produce Champagne by the traditional *méthode Champenoise* at their recently opened Frankenmuth winery.

**Tabor Hill/Chi Co,** Rt 2, Box 270, Buchanan, Mi 49107.
Founded 1970. Owner, David Upton; winemaker, Leonard Olson. Storage capacity 60,000 gallons. Produces table wine under brand name Tabor Hill.

**Vendramino Vineyards Co,** Rt 1, Box 257, Paw Paw, Mi 49079.
Founded 1976. Owner, John J Coleman; winemaker, M J Coleman. Storage capacity 5,000 gallons. Produces table wine under brand name Vendramino Vineyards.

**Warner Vineyards,** Paw Paw, Mi.
This winery, claiming to be the largest in the Midwest, provides ample evidence of Michigan's confidence in itself as a wine-producing state. Since 1958 when, as Michigan Wineries, it was bought by the Warner family it has expanded and introduced innovations and is currently spending millions of dollars in development and new equipment including 20,000 gallon storage and fermentation tanks. It makes its champagne by the traditional French *méthode Champenoise* and, more unusual, its sherries and ports by the *solera* system (see page 43). Each *solera*-produced wine has, in fact, part of the original 1946 vintage in it. Since 1971 it has been growing its own grapes on its 300 acres of vineyards, much of which have been planted with French hybrids, but also buys grapes from over 450 independent growers. Visitors to the winery are entertained by an audio-visual presentation in an old Grand Trunk railroad car converted into a theater and can sample wines in the Wine Haus which, ironically, began life as the Paw Paw waterworks. Warner's winemaker is Mike Byrne and he has recently introduced a white table wine called Liebestrauben which is a blend of 30 percent Seyval Blanc, 29 percent Vidal Blanc, 20 percent Johannisberg Riesling, 11 percent Muscat with 10 percent unfermented Vidal Blanc juice added at the end. It won a Silver Medal in Vienna, Austria in 1980. Another proprietary white wine is L'Aurore Superior made mainly from Aurora grapes. The winery's Champagnes are marketed under the label Pol Pereaux Champagnes – brut, extra dry and pink – and there is also a Pol Pereaux Cold Duck. Capriccio Spumante is a sparkling semisweet wine (Gold Medal Amsterdam 1980).

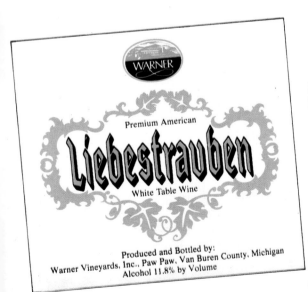

WARNER

Premium American

**Liebestrauben**

White Table Wine

Produced and Bottled by:
Warner Vineyards, Inc., Paw Paw, Van Buren County, Michigan
Alcohol 11.8% by Volume

There is also a whole range of Cask wines — including Sherries and Ports, a King Solomon Kosher wine and Cask champagnes. Premium wines include: Seyval Blanc, Johannisberg Riesling, Chardonnay, Chancellor Noir, Cabernet Sauvignon and Vineyard Red.

How big can they get? A storage barrel at the Warner Valley Vineyard and Winery in Paw Paw, Michigan.

WARNER
MICHIGAN
Champagne
BRUT
Naturally Fermented in this Bottle
Cellared and Bottled at the winery by Warner Vineyards
Paw Paw, Van Buren County, Michigan
Alcohol 12% by volume

POL PEREAUX
American
BRUT CHAMPAGNE
Charmat Bulk Process
Naturally Fermented Sparkling Wine
ALCOHOL 12% BY VOLUME
Cellared and bottled at the winery by Pol Pereaux Champagne Cellars
Paw Paw, Van Buren County, Michigan.

WARNER
PREMIUM MICHIGAN
Chancellor Noir
Produced and bottled by
Warner Vineyards, Inc.
Paw Paw, Van Buren County, Michigan
Alcohol 12% by volume

A mechanical harvester gathering grapes in
Warner Vineyard.

161

## MARYLAND

**Boordy Vineyards Inc,** Hydes, Md 21082.

Boordy was founded by Philip and Jocelyn Wagner, his wife and collaborator in the vineyard, in 1945. Philip Wagner, a winemaker of high repute and the author of books on wine — *American Wines and How to Make Them* and *American Wines and Winemaking* — foretold as early as 1955 that vine-growing in every part of the United States would be revolutionized following the introduction of French hybrid grapes and he has proved to be right. Under his sway Boordy, a small winery, achieved, not surprisingly, a high reputation and in 1980 it passed into the hands of the present owners, the R B Deford Family who were not only friends of the Wagners but had grown grapes for them. The winemaker now is Robert Deford III who studied enology and viticulture at that famous *alma mater* of winemakers, the University of California, Davis. The Defords are clearly determined to continue the tradition of the Wagners. Their capacity remains modest by present standards with a production of 16,000 gallons annually from grapes supplied by six Maryland growers and their own small vineyards near the winery. This is in a 19th-century stone and wood barn on their farm in northeastern Baltimore County. Their standard wines are Maryland Red, Maryland White and Maryland Rosé and their Speciality products Cedar Point Red; 'Nouveau,' a red wine bottled each year on 15 November and so, says the winemaker, 'its youth has been trapped by early bottling and it is best enjoyed within its first year'; and Seyval Blanc.

**Provenza Vineyards,** 805 Greenbridge Road, Brookeville, Md 20833.

Tom and Barbara Provenza, owners of this small 15-acre vineyard, bought it in the late 1960s having been home winemakers for some time. They sought the advice of

First steps in the processing of red grapes at Provenza vineyards in Maryland.

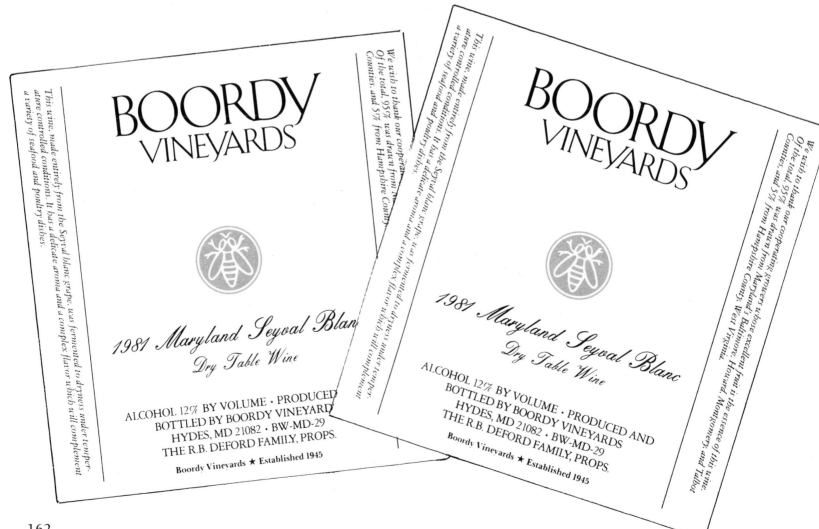

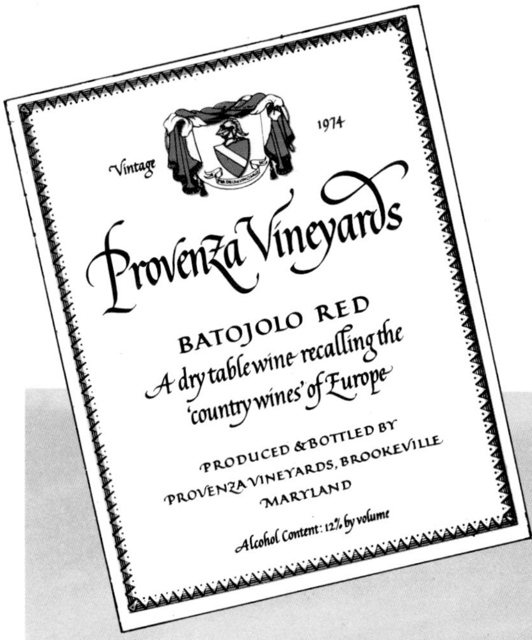

Provenza Vineyards

Vintage 1974

BATOJOLO RED
A dry table wine recalling the
'country wines' of Europe

PRODUCED & BOTTLED BY
PROVENZA VINEYARDS, BROOKEVILLE
MARYLAND

Alcohol Content: 12% by volume

Maryland's best-known winemaker Philip Wagner (see above entry) and between 1970 and 1973 planted French hybrid grapes as was being done generally throughout the country. The vines made an uneasy start but grape growers John and Lee Paul in upper Montgomery County were brought in to help and in 1974 the Provenzas, who had meanwhile built a Swiss-chalet style winery, produced their first table wine. Current capacity is 8,000 gallons but there is room to expand to 30,000 and the winery produces a variety of dry red, white and rosé table wines.

Left: Hand harvesting at Provenza Vineyard.

Provenza Vineyards, Brookeville, Maryland.

Winter pruning can be a lonely job.

## OHIO

All the famous names in North American wine history are not confined to California and New York. Indeed one of the most distinguished is that of a New England lawyer, Nicholas Longworth, who practiced in the Cincinnatti area of South Ohio. He was not the first to introduce wine to Ohio – here once again the credit goes to the Church for it was Moravian missionaries working with the Delaware Indians who brought native vines into the State. But Longworth certainly had considerable influence encouraging German immigrants and made Ohio an important wine state in the 19th century. As early as 1825 he introduced the North American (North Carolina) native Catawba grape to his vineyard in the Cincinatti area believing that it could stand the climatic extremes there. He was right. The Catawba made a light, semisweet wine, not as strong as the American wines of the period, and it soon became so popular that by 1845 over 300,000 gallons were being produced every year. It was of this wine that Longfellow wrote:

> 'But Catawba wine
> Has a taste more divine
> More dulcet, delicious and dreamy.'

In 1847 Longworth discovered an accidental secondary fermentation in a bottle and from this resulted Sparkling Catawba, America's first Champagne.

Making wine had become so important that as early as 1851 Ohio had its first American Wine Growers Association to set and maintain standards. Catawba wine remained popular until Prohibition but by then Longworth's Cincinatti vineyards had long disappeared as the city grew, and disease, the Civil War and other calamities brought a virtual end to wine production in the south of the State with Ohio ceasing to be the leading wine state – a role taken over by California. Meanwhile grape growing and winemaking had developed in the north of the state along the climatically kinder southern shore of Lake Erie and some islands in the Lake and by the beginning of the present century 5,000,000 gallons of wine were being produced in the area by 15 wineries. The wineries suffered serious decline because of Prohibition and by the end of World War II only three wineries still existed. It was not until the 1960s that there was a revival, typical of the resurgence of the wine industry in other states. Helped by the Ohio Agricultural Research and Development Center, which has courses in viticulture and advanced enology, and Ohio State University, Franco-American hybrid grapes were planted in the southern part of the state and, once the experiment had proved successful, in the north. Some indication of the resurgence is provided by the fact that 23 new wineries have been established in the state since 1965 while older wineries have expanded. It must be admitted that many of the new wineries are very small, but they are a hopeful sign for the future.

Two of the oldest surviving wineries are the Lonz Winery on Middle Bass Island in Lake Erie, which was first opened during the Civil War, and Meier's Wine Cellars which has been in the business for over 100 years and which now owns Lonz. Meier's with its headquarters in Silverton, Cincinatti, and with a capacity of 2,500,000 gallons annually, also has its vineyards on a Lake Erie Island. It once belonged to Canada and was known as Ile St George but it is now called Bass Island although Meier's still use Ile St George on their labels. The island's microclimates are said to give a growing season six weeks longer than that on the mainland with a late bud-break because of intense winter cold but a longer fall maturing period.

Out of 20,000 tons of grapes produced in the State annually 7,000 to 8,000 tons go to the making of wine. Most important of the native grape varieties is still the Catawba but others, apart from French hybrids and *vinifera* grapes, are the Delaware, Niagara and Ives Seedling.

**Au Provence – Cedar Hill Wine Company**, 2195 Lee Road, Cleveland Heights, Oh 321-9511.

Winery or restaurant? That is the question. In fact the answer is both. In the basement of the small but elegant restaurant, Au Provence, Dr Tom Wykoff, who is

appropriately a nose and throat surgeon as well as a winemaker, produces some dozen different wines under the label Château Lagniappe. Not surprisingly the winery is small, one of the smallest in the country, but with grapes from the southern shore of Lake Erie and the Finger Lakes of New York he produces wine for the restaurant with some to spare for retail sales. In 1980 they made 22,500 bottles. The doctor's wines include Seyval Blanc, Chardonnay, Riesling, Chambourçin, Pinot Noir and Gamay.

**Brushcreek Vineyards,** Rt 412351, Newkirk Lane, Peebles, Oh 45660.
A southern Ohio family concern – Brush Creek is a tributary of the River Ohio – this small winery operates in a log building over a century and a half old.

**John Christ Winery,** 23421 Walker Road, Avon Lake, Oh 44012.
The winery founded as a small family operation in 1947 has 25 acres of vineyards, virtually on the south shore of Lake Erie. Now run by Alex, son of the founder after whom it is named, it produces traditional American grape wines such as Concord, Niagara, Half-and-Half (a mixture of Concord and Niagara), Pink Catawba and Claret.

**E & K Wine Company,** 220 East Water Street, Sandusky, Oh 44870.
Another small winery featuring traditional American grape wines such as Concord, Catawba, Niagara and Delaware. A special blend is called Mellow Monk.

**Heritage Vineyards,** 6020 Wheelock St, W Milton, Oh 45363.
There are 20 acres of vineyard growing 12,000 vines alongside the winery which is about 20 miles north of Dayton. The winery produces 15 different wines, some from native eastern US grapes such as Niagara (sweet white), Delaware Rosé, Light Red Concord and Red Catawba. Others are from French hybrids and include Heritage Vin Blanc, Seyval Blanc, De Chaunac, Maréchal Foch, Chelois and Baco Noir.

**Lonz Winery,** Middle Bass Island, Oh 43446.
Started as the Golden Eagle Winery during the Civil War, this was by 1875 the largest wine producer in the United States. Now owned by Meier's Wine Cellars Inc it continues to produce the fine quality wines for which it has been known.

**Markko Vineyard,** Rt 2 South Ridge Road, Conneaut, Oh 44030.
Situated on the very far northeast corner of the State, almost on the Pennsylvania State line, this vineyard and winery was founded in 1968 by Arnulf Esterer (the winemaker) and Tim Hubbard. The vineyard covers only 10 acres and is planted

Opposite: The interior of the Au Provence Restaurant above the winery at Cleveland Heights, Ohio.

**Isle St. George**
**Haut Sauternes**

A semi-sweet, fruity white wine

Produced and Bottled by Meier's Wine Cellars, Inc., Silverton, Ohio
Alcohol 12% by Volume

with White Riesling (40 percent), Chardonnay (40 percent) and Cabernet Sauvignon (20 percent) grapes. The partners acknowledge gratefully that they had guidance from the distinguished enologist, Dr Konstantin Frank, pioneer in the growing of *vinifera* grapes in the Finger Lakes region of New York. They, too, have concentrated on the *vinifera* on Lake Erie's southern ridge. Markko produces Riesling and Chardonnay and a Cabernet Sauvignon which is a blend of that grape and a French hybrid Chambourçin. They also have two jug table wines — a non-vintage Riesling, Chardonnay or a blend of both.

**Meier's Wine Cellars Inc,** Silverton, Cincinatti, Oh 45236.

This is the headquarters of Ohio's largest and most prestigious winery. Although you may enjoy the attractive gardens you will not see any grapes growing because the headquarters are only 10 minutes from downtown Cincinatti. It is a reminder that when Meier's was established over a century ago the city was still the center of the Ohio wine industry, then the largest in the country. Meier's 350 acres of vineyards are on Bass Island, one of a cluster of islands in Lake Erie known as 'the wine islands', and the concern has another winery at Sandusky on the Lake Erie shore almost opposite the island. Although the vineyards cover only 350 acres Meier's own the whole of Bass Island which extends for 740 acres. The growing season for grapes here is six weeks longer than on the mainland. Grapes have been grown there for nearly 140 years. Meier's started toward the end of the last century and gradually acquired more and more small vineyards on Bass Island. Today their 350 acres supply them with 1,500 to 2,000 tons annually. Meier's itself was bought by Robert Gottesman, owner of Paramount Distillers, in 1976 and they now own Lonz Winery on Middle Bass Island. Although much of the output is still made from traditional North American grapes such as Catawba, Concord, Delaware, and Diamont, there has been much replacement by French hybrids and *vinifera* stocks. Some 8,000 *vinifera* were planted in 1976 and another 12,000 in 1978. Their list of wines is impressive indeed and includes a Blanc de Blanc Champagne (made by the Charmat bulk process), Ile St George Johannisberg Riesling, Haut Sauternes, Chardonnay, Gewürztraminer, Pale Dry Cocktail Sherry, Rich Golden Sherry and Light Cream Sherry, white, tawny and ruby Port, and Catawba — to name a few.

**Moyer Vineyards Winery and Restaurant,** US Route 52, Manchester, Oh.

Another small combined operation on the River Ohio, almost in Kentucky. It produces Moyer Natural and River Valley Wines and Brut Champagne made by the *méthode Champenoise.*

170

**Steuk Wine Company,** 1001 Fremont, Sandusky, Oh 44871.
Another winery that concentrates on traditional American grape wines, Steuk has been a family wine concern for a century and a quarter. The majority of its wines are made from Concord, Delaware, Catawba and Black Pearl grapes.

**Stone Quarry Vineyards Winery,** Mill St, Box 142, Waterford, Oh 45786.
Almost on the border of West Virginia this small winery produces French hybrid and American wines aged in American oak barrels.

**Valley Vineyards,** 2041 East US 22 & 23, Morrow, Oh 45152.
Here are 45 acres of vineyards in the Little River Valley of Southern Ohio planted with French hybrids and American grapes producing wines aged in small oak casks and stainless-steel tanks.

## SOUTHERN STATES

Winemaking in the Southern States can hardly be regarded as a significant industry but as elsewhere there are abundant signs of growing interest. One winery, the Rushing Winery in Marigold, Mississippi produces some 15,000 gallons annually of wine from native Muscat grapes; Virginia has 16 vineyards and in the eight southeastern states there are now 21 wineries. Most of them are new and small and are insignificant in the context of the national wine production scene. Nevertheless they are there and are symptomatic of a general trend. Perhaps the most significant of them is:

**Truluck Vineyards,** PO Drawer 1265, Route 3, Lake City, SC 29560.
This winery and vineyard is on the estate of the Truluck family on the outskirts of Lake City which is some 80 miles north of Charleston. James P Truluck Jr, who founded the concern, is a dental doctor and if he had not served for a time in the US Air Force Dental Corps in the Loire Valley in France in the late 1950s the winery probably would not exist. In fact two things happened. Dr Truluck developed a taste for and an interest in wine and comparing geographical and climatic conditions came to the conclusion that, using the right grapes, comparable wine could be made at Lake City. In 1960 when he returned home he sought advice and was told that only native Concord and Muscat grapes could be grown successfully, but he was not convinced and in 1972 he and his wife Kay planted French hybrid grapes on the family estate. They bought them, incidentally, from that veteran winemaker Philip Wagner of Boordy Vineyards (p 162). Today on 100 acres of vineyards they have 300 varieties of grapes, some in the early experimental stage. Dr Truluck still practices dentistry

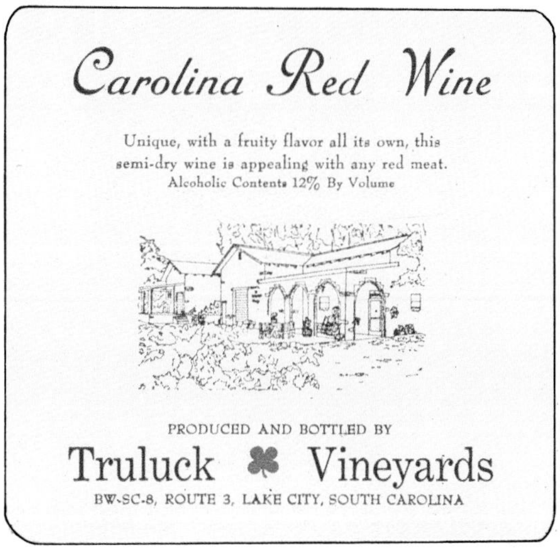

*Rosé de Chambourcin*
A delightful, fruity rose' wine, so very common in Europe. Made from the free run juice of the Chambourcin grape, fermented cold to insure the floral aroma of the grape.
Alcoholic Contents 11.5% By Volume

PRODUCED AND BOTTLED BY
**Truluck ☘ Vineyards**
BW-SC-8, ROUTE 3, LAKE CITY, SOUTH CAROLINA

*Carolina Red Wine*
Unique, with a fruity flavor all its own, this semi-dry wine is appealing with any red meat.
Alcoholic Contents 12% By Volume

PRODUCED AND BOTTLED BY
**Truluck ☘ Vineyards**
BW-SC-8, ROUTE 3, LAKE CITY, SOUTH CAROLINA

SOUTH CAROLINA
*Cayuga White*
**1981**
A well balanced white wine, slightly dry with a distinctive varietal character.
Alcoholic Contents 12% By Volume

PRODUCED AND BOTTLED BY
**Truluck ☘ Vineyards**
BW-SC-8, ROUTE 3, LAKE CITY, SOUTH CAROLINA, U.S.A.

171

but his wife manages the winery and is helped by two sons and a daughter. Their selection of premium wines covers: Carolina Red, Rosé and White; Carlos; Ravat Blanc; Villard Blanc; Chambourcin; Munson Red; Cayuga White; Golden Muscat; Seyval Blanc; Rosé de Chambourçin; Vidal Blanc. The last, a crisp, semidry white wine is happily described on the label as 'appropriate anytime.'

## VIRGINIA

Virginia has a curious wine history. It was one of the first, if not the first, of the states to start winemaking in 1616 which was only 13 years after the death of Queen Elizabeth I, the Virgin Queen, after whom it is named. It was in that year that Lord De La Warr, Governor of the State, had the Virginia Company in London send out vine cuttings to the colony. This was despite the fact that there were plenty of native North American of the foxy variety around. Regrettably his experiment was not particularly successful and little was heard of Virginia as a wine-producing state until today, although George Washington had a vineyard at Mount Vernon and Thomas Jefferson one at Monticello, and Virginia 'claret' had some reputation a century ago.

Today Virginia is low in the wine-producing table, but there are many signs of expansion. In the 1960s there was hardly a winery in sight as it were. Today there are 16 estate wineries, that is with their own vineyards, all started in the second half of the 1970s and with another five to come into operation. The largest of the 16 has 45 acres of vineyards, the smallest four and a half. Some have not yet produced their first wines commercially. Four viticultural areas have been proposed for the State — Monticello, Rocky Knob, Shenandoah Valley and North Fork of the Roanoke. Wine festivals are already a feature of activity in Virginia.

In the southern style the house of the Ingleside Plantation Vineyard.

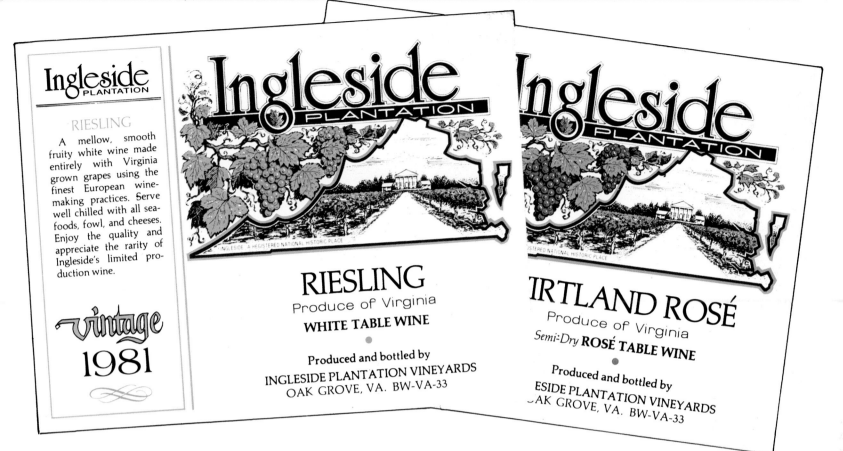

Ingleside PLANTATION

RIESLING

A mellow, smooth fruity white wine made entirely with Virginia grown grapes using the finest European wine-making practices. Serve well chilled with all sea-foods, fowl, and cheeses. Enjoy the quality and appreciate the rarity of Ingleside's limited pro-duction wine.

*vintage* 1981

RIESLING
Produce of Virginia
**WHITE TABLE WINE**
•
Produced and bottled by
INGLESIDE PLANTATION VINEYARDS
OAK GROVE, VA. BW-VA-33

IRTLAND ROSÉ
Produce of Virginia
*Semi-Dry* **ROSÉ TABLE WINE**
•
Produced and bottled by
ESIDE PLANTATION VINEYARDS
AK GROVE, VA. BW-VA-33

**Bacchanal Vineyards,** Route 2, Box 860, Afton, Va 22920.
Owner: David Mefford. Six acres of vineyard planted in 1978 with Chenin Blanc, Zinfandel, Gewürztraminer, Sémillon, Pinot Noir, Chardonnay, Riesling and Cabernet Sauvignon.

**Barboursville Vineyard,** PO Box F, Barboursville, Va 22923.
Owners: Zonin Gambellara SpA. 32 acres of vineyard planted in 1976. Wines available are Cabernet Sauvignon, Chardonnay, White Riesling, Rosé Barboursville, Merlot, Gewürztraminer.

**Farfelu Vineyards,** Highway 647, Flint Hill, Va 22627.
Owners: Charles J Raney family. First vines planted 1967. 33 acres now under grapes. Wines available include Cayuga White, Dry Red Leon Millot (a dry red varietal), and Seyval Blanc. Annual production 2,500 gallons.

**Ingleside Plantation Vineyards,** PO Box 1038, Oak Grove, Va.
President: Carl F Flemer Jr. Present vineyard area 20 acres, close to birthplaces of George Washington and Robert E Lee. Vineyard is being extended; winery has 20,000 gallons capacity. Wines available are in reds, Cabernet Sauvignon, Chancellor, Nouveau Red, Roxbury Red; in whites, Aurora, Chardonnay, Ingleside Fraulein, Ingleside White, Riesling, Seyval Blanc; there are also a Wirtland Rosé and a semidry Virginia Champagne.

**Mountain Cove Vineyards/La Abra Farm and Winery Inc,** RFD 1, Box 139, Lovingston, Va 22949.
The vineyards cover 12 acres under French hybrid grapes producing Villard Blanc, Skyline White, Skyline Red and a semidry rosé made from Chelois grapes.

**Meredyth Vineyards,** PO Box 347, Middleburg, Va 22117.
President: Archie M Smith. Largest of the estate wineries and started in the early 1970s, its 45 acres of vineyards produce about 20,000 gallons of wine annually. They are Aurora Blanc, de Chaunac, Maréchal Foch, Riesling, Rougeon Rosé, Seyval Blanc, Villard Blanc, Villard Noir.

Ingleside PLANTATION

*Virginia*
**Champagne**
DRY

Bottled and Fermented in this Bottle by
**INGLESIDE PLANTATION VINEYARDS**
OAK GROVE, VA
Alc. 12% by vol.

The vineyard of Montdomaine Cellars Inc in Charlottesville, Virginia.

**MJC Vineyard,** Rt 1, Box 293, Blacksburg, Va 24060.
Owners: Karl and Myra Hereford. 15 acres of vineyards planted in 1972 with *vinifera* and hybrid grapes. Winery has a capacity of 12,000 gallons annually. Wines produced, under Pearis label, red, white and rosé wines from Maréchal Foch, Chambourçin, Seyval and Vidal grapes. Under the Appalachian Harvest label a light, sweet wine from Delaware, Dutchess and Aurora grapes. For release 1983, varietals Merlot, Sauvignon Blanc, Chardonnay and Pinot Noir.

**Montdomaine Cellars Inc,** Rt 6, Box 168A, Charlottesville, Va 22901.
President: Michael E Bowles. Has 20 acres of vineyards under Chardonnay, Merlot and Cabernet Sauvignon with a further 10 acres being planted. A new winery with over 80,000-bottle capacity is under construction. Wines available are estate-bottled Chardonnay and Merlot, aged in oak.

**Naked Mountain Vineyard,** PO Box 131, Markham, Va 22643.
Co-owners: Bob and Phoebe Harper. Smallest of the Virginia wineries, the vineyard covers four and a half acres, was planted in 1976 and the first wines produced in 1981. They are Chardonnay, Gewürztraminer, Sauvignon Blanc, Riesling, all 100 percent varietals and a 'claret' made from Merlot, Cabernet Sauvignon and Cabernet Franc grapes.

**Oasis Vineyards,** Highway 635, Hume, Va 22639.
Owner: Dirgham Salahi. Planted only in 1977 and 1978 the 30 acres of vineyards,

with a newly designed winery, will have an annual capacity of 50,000 gallons. Wines already produced in limited quantities are Sauvignon Blanc, Riesling, Gewürztraminer, Chardonnay, Seyval Blanc and Rayon d'Or in whites and Cabernet Sauvignon, Merlot, Pinot Noir, Chancellor and Chelois in red.

**Piedmont Vineyards and Winery Inc,** Highway 626 South, PO Box 286, Middlesburgh, Va 22117.
Owner: Mrs Thomas Furness. Winemaker: Walter Luchsinger, University of California, Davis trained enologist. Founded 1973. The vineyard covers 30 acres planted mainly with Chardonnay and Sémillon grapes and there is a new winery equipped entirely with modern stainless-steel fittings. Eventual production 20,000 gallons annually. Wines produced include Virginia Chardonnay, Virginia Sémillon, Virginia Seyval Blanc.

**Rapidan River Vineyards,** Rt 4, Box 199, Culpeper, Va 22701.
Owners: Dr and Mrs Gerhard W R Guth. Winemaker and vineyard manager: Joachim Hollerith. Founded only in 1978 there are 25 acres of vineyards planted with 27,000 vines. The wines are made according to the German tradition – the winemaker has a degree in viticulture and enology from Geisenheim University – and are White Riesling, Chardonnay, Gewürztraminer and Pinot Noir.

**Rose Bower Vineyard and Winery,** PO Box 126, Hampden-Sydney, Va 23943.
Owners: Tom and Bronwyn O'Grady. The next to smallest in the state, the vineyard covers only six acres and was started in 1974. Wines produced are Foch Nouveau, a dry red made from 100 percent Maréchal Foch grapes, Hampden Forest, a dry 'claret,' Johannisberg Riesling (botrytized), Pinot Chardonnay, Cabernet Sauvignon and Le Bon Sauvage, a blended white wine.

**Shenandoah Vineyards,** 208B, Route 2, Edinburg, Va 22824.
Owners: James B and Emma Randel. Winemaker: Alan Kinne. Licensed only in 1977 with 10 acres of French American hybrids and eight of *vinifera*, the winery already produces Chambourçin, Chancellor, Seyval Blanc, Shenandoah Blanc, a medium-dry white, Shenandoah Rosé and Vidal Blanc.

**Tri-Mountain Winery and Vineyards Inc,** Rt 1, Box 254, Middletown, Va 22645.
President: Joseph C Geraci. Another child of the early 1970s the first wines were produced in 1981 from its 13 acres of vineyard (another 10 are to be planted). Annual production is 7,000 gallons. Wines already produced include Blue Ridge Rosé, Great North Mountain Concord, Massanutten White and Tri-Mountain Red.

**Woolwine Winery and Weathervane Vineyards,** Box 100, Woolwine, Va 24185
Owner: William F Morrisette. One of the youngest of the Virginia wineries, Woolwine was started in 1976 with 17 acres of French hybrids and *vinifera* grapes. Its first wines are due on the market in 1983 and 1984.

Virginia wineries newly licensed or about to be:
**Blenheim Wine Cellars Ltd,** Rt 6, Box 75, Charlottesville, Va 22901.
10.5 acres of Chardonnay, Riesling and Merlot.
**Château Naturel Vineyard,** Rocky Mount, Va 24151.
Eight acres of French hybrids.
**Chermont Winery Inc,** Rt 1, Box 59, Esmont, Va 22937.
Four acres Chardonnay, five acres Riesling, one acre Cabernet Sauvignon.
**Domaine de Gignoux,** Box 48, Ivy, Va 22945.
Four acres of Chardonnay, Cabernet Sauvignon, Cabernet Franc and Merlot.
**Oakencraft Vineyards,** Rt 5, Charlottesville, Va 22901.
Seven acres of Seyval Blanc, Chardonnay and Merlot.

# CHAPTER SEVEN
## Canada

In contrast to the rest of North America the wine history of Canada has been uninterrupted in that it did not suffer the disastrous effects of Prohibition. In fact, with those 3,000 plus miles of undefended frontier, Canadian wineries probably benefited to some extent from their neighbors' misfortune. In view of the obvious climatic disadvantages (from a winemaking point of view) of the Dominion it is hardly surprising that the wine industry of Canada is on a limited scale. Although it is known that in the 17th century French colonists made wine from native grapes as did Jesuit missionaries for sacramental and more personal requirements, the first record of the commercial cultivation of the grape for wine production dates back to 1811. Then a German named Johann Schiller established a small winery at Cooksville on the Credit River which flows into Lake Ontario just south of Toronto. It is the area south of this, the Niagara Peninsula between Lakes Ontario and Erie, where there are 20,000 acres of vineyards, that is still the center of the Canadian wine industry. The annual grape yield exceeds 50,000 tons. Wine grapes are also grown and wine produced in British Columbia, particularly in the Okanagau Valley, and there are wineries today in at least five other provinces — Alberta, Manitoba, New Brunswick, Nova Scotia and Quebec.

Tipping out grapes for one of the White Wines of Château-Gai in Mississauga, Ontario.

Previous page: Transplanted vine cuttings in a 'polyhouse' at Brights, Niagara Falls, Ontario.

The industry produces almost every type of wine — apéritifs (sherry and vermouths), white table wines such as Sauternes and Rieslings, red table wines described as Canadian claret and Burgundy, rosés, dessert wines (sherries and port), Canadian Tokay and Muscatel, 'crackling' or pétillant wines and Canadian sparkling wines including Champagne. Canadian wine drinkers in recent years have followed the general trend in North America, turning to the more sophisticated drier table wines and the leading wineries are proud of the fact that some of their best products are not only sold in Europe but have won prizes there.

Canada's oldest surviving winery is that of Barnes, founded on the banks of the Welland Canal at St Catharines, Ontario in 1873. The following year Brights by the Niagara Falls was established and is still a flourishing concern. The next oldest survivor is the evocatively named Château-Gai at Stamford, Niagara Falls, founded some 16 years later. Two leading present-day wineries, Jordan & Ste Michelle and Andrés were founded in 1921 and 1961 respectively and although their headquarters are on the Niagara Peninsula they have wineries in other provinces including British Columbia. If the growing interest in the more sophisticated types of wine and the developments consequent on it which are the feature of the United States wine scene are duplicated in Canada, there is a big future for the industry. Climatic conditions in the larger part of the Dominion must obviously limit the growth of suitable wine grapes but Canada is a big country and with the vast increase in viticultural knowledge and improved scientific know-how in the actual making of wines it would be surprising if the industry were not to expand rapidly. One winery has invested over $8,000,000 in the past three years in improving its production facilities. The demand is certainly there. In the last decade wine consumption per capita increased from 0.8 gallons to 1.7 gallons, or perhaps a more convincing statistic is that retail wine sales quadrupled from $100,000,000 to $400,000,000. Canadian produced wines account for the majority of wines consumed in the Dominion but 40 percent is still imported — a tempting target for Canadian producers.

One of the largest and most vigorous of the Canadian wine-producing concerns attributes the recent growth of the industry to: 'increased prosperity of Canadian consumers; the growing sophistication in our life style; the growing interest in wine and knowledge about wine; increased travel abroad by Canadians exposing them to wine; the surge in European immigration which has meant many new Canadians with an established taste for wine; a shift in Canadian taste preferences away from harsher tasting alcoholic beverages towards lighter tasting wines; the high price of many imported wines giving Canadian wines a substantial price advantage; and, most important, the steadily improving quality of Canadian wines as a result of viticultural research and advances in winemaking technology.' To the wine drinker used to the familiar and comparatively simple European geographical labels such

as Chablis or Côtes du Rhône brand names such as Botticelli, Auberge, Fiorino, Richelieu, Galante, Coffee Cream, Eagle Ridge, Moody Blue or Very Cold Duck are perhaps difficult to swallow. This does not mean that the wines themselves are difficult to swallow — very much the reverse. As has been mentioned, more than one Canadian winery can boast of winning gold, silver and bronze medals in international competitions, many of them in Europe.

**Andrés,** PO Box 550 (Kelson Avenue and QEW), Winona, Ontario.
Although its headquarters are now at Winona in the Niagara Peninsula, Andrés began life in British Columbia when Andrew (hence André) Peller started a winery at Port Moody in 1961. Within three years he had established other wineries in Alberta, Calgary and in Truro, Nova Scotia. In 1970 he returned to the Niagara Peninsula (where he had formerly had a successful brewery) and there he bought Beau Chatel Wines in Winona. Since then he has founded Les Vins Andrés de Quebec at St Hyacinthe and the Valley Rouge Winery in Morris, Manitoba. The range of the firm's products is little short of fantastic although the emphasis is on fine sparkling and table wines. Its Baby Duck, a low alcohol content (seven percent) blend of

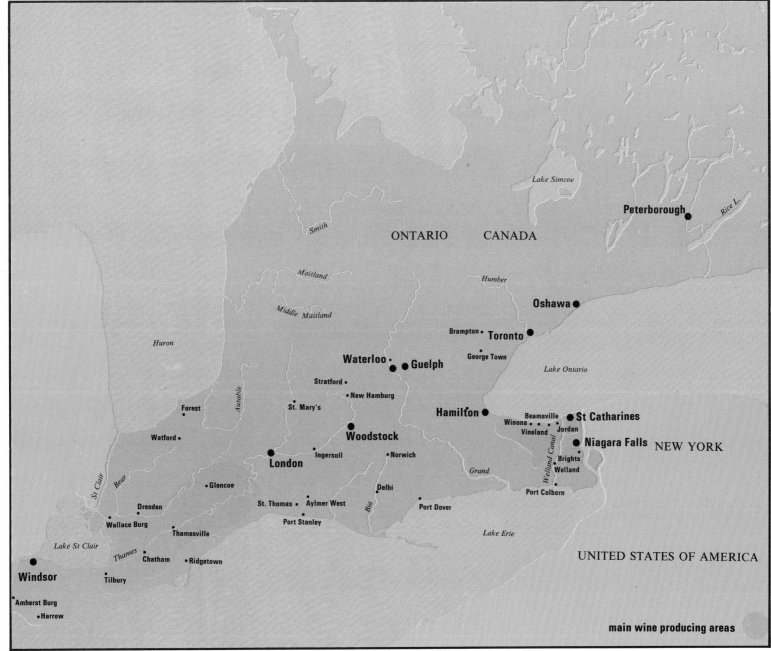

main wine producing areas

RICHELIEU
Pink Canadian Champagne
Canadian Champagne Canadien
750 ml   11.5% alc./vol.
Andrés Wines Ltd., Winona, Canada

ANDRES

750 ml                    7% alc./vol.

CORDOBA
BLANCA

PRODUCT OF CANADA    PRODUIT DU CANADA
ANDRÉS WINES LTD., WINONA, CANADA
SPARKLING WHITE WINE/VIN BLANC SEC

RED·WINE·VIN·ROUGE

BOTTICELLI
SOFT, SEMI-DRY RED WINE

750 ml                    9% alc./vol.

Andrés Wines Ltd., Winona, Canada
PRODUCT OF CANADA/PRODUIT DU CANADA

ANDRES

Auberge

DRY WHITE WINE / VIN BLANC SEC

The wine of the "Auberge" or "Inn" has been
historically viewed as a simple, pleasant, good quality wine.
In this tradition Andrés offers Auberge...an enjoyable, medium
dry white wine produced to serve as your house wine.

Andrés Wines Ltd., Winona, Canada
PRODUCT OF CANADA/PRODUIT DU CANADA

11.5% alc./vol.                    1.5 L

ANDRES

750 ml                    7% alc./vol.

Baby Bubbly
Red

A Light                      Vin Rouge
Sparkling Red Wine      Léger et Mousseux

Medium Dry • Demi Sec

ANDRES WINES LTD., WINONA, CANADA

Cold Duckling
SPARKLING      MOUSSEUX

Selection and blend of light mellow
red & white sparkling wines.
Un mélange de vins rouge & blancs
de qualité léger et mousseux.
7% alc./vol.                    750 ml
ANDRES WINES LTD., WINONA, CANADA
PRODUCT OF CANADA/PRODUIT DU CANADA

SPARKLING WINE

375ml                    7% alc./vol.

BABY DUCK

Le vin mousseux de      The quality sparkling
qualité au goût et        wine with unique
au caractère unique      taste and character

ANDRES WINES LTD., WINONA, CANADA
PRODUCT OF CANADA/PRODUIT DU CANADA

ANDRES

RICHELIEU

BACO NOIR

Richelieu Baco Noir represents the highest level of excellence
in Andrés winemaking. Truly an historic achievement in
viticultural technology, this red hybrid grape of European
ancestry is full bodied and extremely rich in bouquet and
flavour. The 1979 vintage has been produced entirely from
select Ontario grown Baco Noir grapes and is available
in very limited quantity.

SPECIAL 1979 VINTAGE
LIMITED BOTTLING   No   11180
750 ml                    11.5% alc./vol.
PRODUCED & BOTTLED BY ANDRES WINES LTD., WINONA, CANADA

Moody
Blue

ANDRES

HOUSE WINE

VIN ROUGE          RED WINE

House Wines from Andrés represent the fruits of the pains-
taking labours of the Andrés winemaker. Beginning with the
selection of premium French hybrid grapes, the winemaker
supervises the pressing, fermentation and finishing of this
quality wine. The result, Andrés House Wine, a unique, dry
red wine with beaujolais-like colour and bouquet...light in
body, rich in character.

1.5 L
11.5% alc./vol.
Andrés Wines Ltd., Winona, Canada
PRODUCT OF CANADA / PRODUIT DU CANADA

ANDRES

750 ml                    19% alc./vol.

RICHELIEU
Golden Cream
CANADIAN SHERRY
VIN · WINE

A superior sherry slowly aged in oak casks.

PRODUCT OF CANADA          PRODUIT DU CANADA
PRODUCED & BOTTLED BY ANDRES WINES LTD., WINONA, CANADA

premium red and white sparkling wines is Canada's largest selling wine — domestic or imported. Its Similkameen Superior, a light dry red wine made from grapes from the Valley of that name in British Columbia, won silver medals three years running at the international wine competition at Llubljana in Yugoslavia. Outstanding among its varietal wines are those sold under the Richelieu label, in reds a Baco Noir from Ontario-grown grapes of that name, and in whites a Pinot Chardonnay, a Vidal, and a Chaunac Blanc, all from Ontario-grown grapes. Andrés' sherries include a Richelieu pale dry with an alcoholic content of 18.5 percent, a Richelieu Golden Cream (19 percent), Coffee Cream (18 percent) and Medium Dry Canadian Sherry (16 percent). Other products include Crackling Rosé, Crackling Vin Blanc, Richelieu Pink Champagne, Richelieu Extra Dry Champagne, Botticelli, a semidry red, Franciscan, a Canadian Chablis, Moulin Rouge, a dry red, Moulin Blanc and Moulin Rosé (all three Gold Medal winners in Sofia, Bulgaria, in 1976), a Richelieu Riesling and countless other exotic names including Moody Blue which is described on the label as a grape wine with natural blueberry flavor added — 'a saucy splash of blueberry superbly refreshing when chilled.' Some of the names are so exuberant that it is quite refreshing to come across a simple label, House Wine. It is perhaps not surprising that Andrés, with its vast range of different types of wine does not have its own vineyards but relies on grape growers for its supplies.

**Barnes Wines Limited,** PO Box 248, St Catharines, Ontario.
It was in 1873 that George Barnes began producing the first Canadian wine commercially at St Catharines, a small town on the Welland Canal which connects Lake Ontario with Lake Erie. The canal had just been enlarged and the new winery stood on its banks. In 1932 the canal was rerouted leaving Barnes Winery high if not dry but still flourishing. In the days of the old canal, ships were towed between the two lakes by teams of mules, a long and somewhat boring process. What should be more natural than that the ships' captains and officers should relieve this boredom by stopping off at Barnes and sampling the wares? What is more it was not just a question of sampling but buying a few bottles to take on their journey. It was a process which spread the winery's reputation and today the same building is still in use producing nearly a score of different wines. As with most Canadian wineries the grapes are not grown in their own vineyards but under contract, in this case from vineyards in the Niagara Peninsula. The winery's list covers: in reds, Weinfest Red, a medium dry from French hybrids and traditional North American grapes; Ontario County Red from French hybrids; Canadian Claret, Bon Appetit Red and Maréchal Foch. In whites there are Weinfest White, a medium dry from Emerald Riesling and Ontario grapes; Ontario County White, extra dry from Muscatel varieties combined

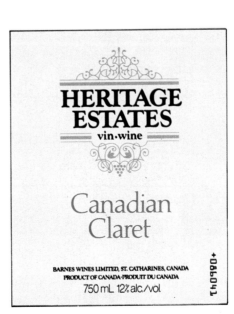

Orderly rows of vines at Brights Vineyards above mean that the harvested grapes from Canada's largest winery require huge trucks.

Right: An even bigger bottling plant for Canada's largest winery.

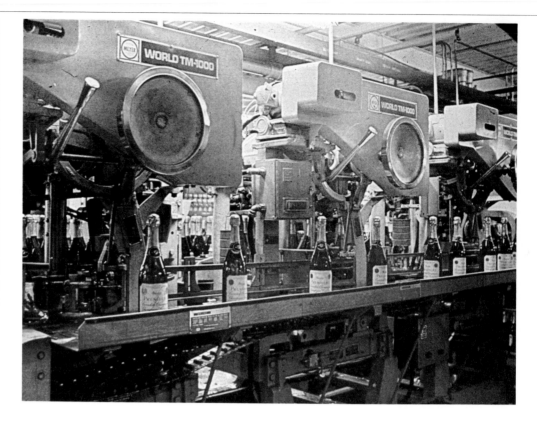

with the Emerald Riesling; Bon Appetit White and a Sauterne from North American grapes. There are two Rosés – Still Cold Duck and Still Rosé; a Grand Celebration Champagne, Cavalier and Cold Duck, both sparkling; and for dessert wines Heritage Sherries – Cream, Dry and Very Pale, Concord Port, made as its name indicates from the traditional North American grape, and a sweet dessert wine called Hostess. Not all wine concerns would be so courageous as to advocate as Barnes Wines does, that Hostess makes an ideal long drink when mixed with ginger ale. Perhaps tastes have changed since the days of the Welland Canal captains.

**Brights or T G Bright & Company Ltd,** POB 510, Niagara Falls, Ontario L2E 6V4. Canada's second oldest surviving winery, Brights also claims to be its largest. It began life in 1874 when T G Bright and F A Shirriff formed a wine company in Toronto and having prospered decided to move 16 years later to the Niagara Peninsula, Canada's main grape-growing area. There, at Stamford near the Niagara Falls, they bought land for vineyards and formed the Niagara Falls Company. In 1910 Shirriff sold his interest to the Brights and the firm became T G Bright and Co Ltd; twenty years later the Brights themselves sold out to Harry C Hatch who kept the name Brights, by then well established. At this time the winery had a capacity of 4,000,000 gallons and was producing four or five brands of wine from *labrusca* grapes. In the 1940s the winery started a big improvement program and in the next 40 years was to spend over $3,000,000 in research and development, importing and experimenting with more than 200 types of wine. The outcome has been the imposing list of wines now produced and an almost equally imposing list of awards, including gold and silver medals in England, Austria, Yugoslavia and other European countries and, of course, the USA. Today its President Canadian Champagne, made by the traditional *méthode Champenoise* and winner of the grand gold medal above all other awards at the Ljubljana International Wine Competition in Yugoslavia in 1979, accounts for two out of three bottles of all champagne, domestic or foreign, sold in Canada. Brights' wines include: President Sauterne; Pinot Chardonnay; White House Wine; Johannisberg Riesling; Seyval Blanc; Entre-Lacs, dry white and red; Gewürztraminer; Warnerhof, a new white wine; Liebesheim, another white; President Burgundy, Villard Noir; de Chaunac; Manor St David's Claret; Baco Noir; Dubarry Sparkling Vin Rosé; and President Muscatel. The winery also produces sweet and dry Sherries and Ports. Mention should also be made of a Sparkling Pink Spumante made from Muscat grapes which is called Pussycat and whose label carries an engaging picture of such an animal who appears to have sampled the contents.

**Château-Gai,** 201 City Center Drive, Mississauga, Ontario.
This is Canada's third oldest surviving winery. A division of Ridout Wines Ltd it was
founded in 1890 in Stamford, just north of the Niagara Falls, as Stamford Park

Wines by a family named Marsh, then became Canadian Wineries Ltd in 1928 and it was not until 1941 that it assumed the name Château-Gai. This was the name of the winery's Champagne, already well known in Canada. The firm, in fact, had bought in 1928 the North American patent for the Charmat method of making sparkling wines with bulk fermentation in sealed tanks and boasts that for a quarter of a century it was Canada's first and only producer of Champagne and sparkling Burgundy. Except for experimental vineyards covering 200 acres in the Niagara Peninsula the winery does not grow its own grapes but buys from local growers. It has modern stainless-steel storage tanks with a capacity of over 1,000,000 gallons and wineries in Scoudouc, New Brunswick and Calgary, Alberta – the first named Château-Gai Wines (Atlantic) and the latter Stoneycroft Cellars, Château-Gai Wines. Its products include Edelwein, a dry 'Rhine style' white wine, Lincoln County Johannisberg Riesling, Pinot Chardonnay (dry white), Gamay Rosé, Capistro, a dry white from California grapes and Alpenweiss, a white wine from a blend of California and Ontario grapes.

**Jordan and Ste Michelle Cellars Limited,** 120 Ridle Road, St Catharines, Ontario. This winery takes its name from a combination of the town on the Niagara Peninsula, Jordan, where the firm began in 1921 and the Ste Michelle Winery in Victoria, British Columbia which began life two years later. Today it has wineries in both places as well as in Calgary, Alberta. Its grapes are grown by private growers under contract in the Niagara Peninsula and the Okanagau Valley, British Columbia. The winery has its own viticulturists who cooperate with the growers to ensure quality and picking is supervised by a resident field manager. It prides itself on combining traditional craftsmanship with modern scientific methods, for example aging its premium red wines and sherries in oak casks and using cold fermentation processes in stainless-steel tanks for their white table wines. The firm produces some 50 different wines, some under a Jordan label, some under Ste Michelle. From Surrey, British Columbia under the Ste Michelle label come Maréchal Foch, a dry red from Gamay and Pinot Noir grapes; a Zinfandel, a Johannisberg Riesling and a Chenin Blanc. Special brand names are Maria Christina (medium white and red), Toscano (dry red and white), Grande Cuvée (dry red and white), Falkenberg (white), Canadian Rhine Castle (white), Jordan Selected Riesling, Jordan Spumante Bambino (sparkling white), Prince de Mousseux (sparkling red and white). Other sparkling brand names include Baby Bear, Sno-Bird, Baby Deer and Lonesome Charlie, with Crackling Rosé, Crackling Perle Blanche and Crackling Cold Duck as pétillants. The winery produce a number of sherries, notably Classic Cream which is also the name of a Canadian port. Jordan and Ste Michelle pride themselves on having won over 150 medals and awards in the past decade, many of them in Europe.

**London Winery Ltd,** 560 Wharncliffe Rd, London, Ontario.
This large winery which has 20 retail stores produces under winemaker Jim Patience
some 50 different wines. It is one of the few North American wineries that uses the
*solera* system in the aging of sherry. Its motto is 'Old World Tradition, New World
Perfection' and certainly its highly modern equipment, stainless-steel fermenting and
storage tanks, laboratory etc are designed to produce the latter.

Far left: Grape picking at the London Winery.

Left: Western Steel storage tanks at the London Winery.

Below: Traditional wooden barrels at the Solera Barrel Cellar of the London Winery.

# CHAPTER EIGHT
## Further Information

It must be confessed that writing a book on the Wines of North America at this stage of the game is both hazardous and intriguing. It is not a simple question, as it used to be, of trying to match European with American wines and methods with a slightly superior attitude toward the former and a tendency to denigrate the latter. As this book, it is hoped, has made clear, many of the wines produced in North America are certainly as good as, and some better than, their equivalents in Europe. The real difficulty is to capture the so-rapidly changing scene, a process involving imagination and a willingness to discard preconceived ideas.

One feature of this North American scene, as readers of the book will have detected, is the rapid appearance of small wineries in unexpected places, in Oregon, Virginia, Ohio and elsewhere. It is easy to dismiss them as the 'Mom and Pop' ventures which many of them are. But so, too, in the beginning were many of the great wine concerns of today, especially in California. After all, the founders of one of the biggest, E & J Gallo, with its 200,000,000-gallon capacity, began in a railroad shed only 50 years ago. Eyrie Vineyards, which scored so signal a success in Beaune, France, in 1980, began with the planting of only 3,000 vine cuttings in 1965. The contrast in the size of vineyards, for example, is grossly deceiving especially where quality is concerned. It is easy to dismiss the 'Mom and Pop' winery with a vineyard acreage of less than 20 to 30 acres when many of the California vineyards extend for thousands of acres. But it is a salutary reminder that some of the world's most renowned wines are produced from comparatively pocket-sized vineyards. Those of the Domaine Comte Georges de Vogüé which produces the famous Musigny extend over less than 40 acres; those of Château la Mission Haut-Brion for only 63 acres; and even of Château Latour only 124 acres. In fact the basic pattern for even the big vineyards in North America seems to be to create a patchwork of smaller vineyards as it were by planting vines of different sorts in the parts of the large vineyards most suitable for them.

The outstanding feature of the wine production is the degree of experimentation, stimulated by increased scientific knowledge, which is taking place. More persistent examination of soil and climatic conditions (microclimates) and of the potentiality and requirements of different types of grape are leading to greater specialization in the wines produced, and it must be said that once a concern is on its feet it seems to encounter little difficulty in raising capital for further development. Which is cause and which is effect it is not always easy to discern but it is clear that changing tastes are playing an increasing part. There is a growing demand for more sophisticated dry table wines but even the bulk wines being produced have moved away from what, as already quoted, a Canadian wine producer described as 'harsher tasting alcoholic beverages.' With all the experimentation, the new wineries are able to install a lot of modern equipment. Many, of course, still adhere to traditional methods, aging in oak casks etc, however some of these still boast of their stainless-steel tanks and other equipment. It is surprising how many North American wineries refer in their publicity to their laboratories, something not at all associated with the vineyards of Europe.

## Learning About Winemaking

One sure sign of the rapid and growing interest in the making of wine in the United States is the increasing number of educational institutions with courses, sometimes to University-degree standard, on viticulture and enology, the study of wine, sometimes spelt oenology. Those with a thirst for knowledge may be interested to know that oenomania is defined in the dictionary as dipsomania; an oenometer as an alcoholometer; and an oenophile, a lover of wine. So if you are an oenophile anxious to become an oenologist the following may be of interest to you. The most famous enology institution is, of course, the University of California at Davis. The reputation of its School of Viticulture and Enology extends beyond North America to Europe and the Antipodes. Indeed even the French, who have been in the game for centuries, recognize the contribution it has made in research and new techniques.

Its assessments of microclimates, soil values, scientific equipment and new methods of harvesting and fermentation, aging and the different qualities of different grapes, have proved invaluable and its alumni are to be found in most of the wine-producing states. Noteworthy also is the contribution by the School of Agricultural Science of the California State University at Fresno with its courses on viticulture and enology.

But California is not alone as the following list shows. It is illustrative rather than exhaustive but indicates clearly the widespread interest:

### Arkansas
The Department of Horticultural Food of its University has a course in grape utilization and enology.

### Colorado State University
This University has viticultural courses at its Agricultural Experiment Station.

### Mississippi
The State University has a degree course in viticulture and enology and a Food and Enology Laboratory.

### Missouri
State University's Department of Horticulture has courses in viticulture and enology.

### New York
The State Agricultural Experiment Station at Geneva has degree programs (including graduate instruction) in viticulture and enology and an extension workshop in winemaking.

### North Carolina
State University has courses in viticulture and enology.

### Ohio
The Ohio Agricultural Research and Development Center at Wooster has courses in viticulture, wine quality and wine examination and enology.

### Pennsylvania
Allentown College, Center Valley has courses in the science of enology.

### Texas
The Technical University at Lubbock has an enology laboratory.

In addition there are many societies which organize serious discussion at periodic or annual meetings. Florida, for example, has an annual Viticultural Science Syndicate and Workshop; Illinois a Midwestern Wine Seminar; the Minnesota Grape Growers' Association organizes seminars through the year; Tennessee has an Annual Conference of its Viticultural and Enological Society. Nationally there is an annual meeting of the American Society of Enologists, Eastern Section, at which technical papers are read.

Canada must not be left out of the picture with the Horticultural Research Institute of Ontario (viticulture and enology), the Grape Growers' School at Vineland Station, Ontario and the Canadian Society of Oenologists at whose annual meeting technical papers are read.

To end on a light note. It is easy for sophisticated winelovers used to the centuries-old European traditional geographic wine names to raise their eyebrows and smile over such North American names as Very Cold Duck, Moody Blue, even Lonesome Charlie. They would do well to remember what the famous English diarist, Samuel Pepys, wrote over 300 years ago after dining at the Royal Oak Tavern in Lombard Street, London. He said they 'drank a sort of French wine called Ho Bryan that hath a good and most particular taste and that I never met with.' What he was drinking, of course, was one of France's most famous wines, Château Haut-Brion but he did not think it was funny that it should be called Ho Bryan, which in name, after all, is not all that different from the Brother O'Brien apéritif wine produced by the Brotherhood Winery in New York State.

ACKNOWLEDGMENTS

We would particularly like to
thank all those who kindly
supplied information, photographs
and labels for this publication.
Unless otherwise indicated below,
the illustrations are from the
Wineries and Vineyards themselves.
Picture research was through

J G Moore Picture Research,
Braceborough, Lincolnshire and,
unless otherwise indicated, all
maps are by Pierre Tilley.

Eastern Grape Grower and Winery
News Magazine, Watkins Glen:
114–115, 116–117, 120–121,
122–123, 130.
Craig Goldwyn, Ithaca: 6–7, 9, 14

(both), 15, 16, 18–19 (both), 22,
22–23, 70–71, 118, 166–167.
Jack Prichett, Berkeley: 10, 26,
44–45, 47, 48, 49, 50.
Roy Williams: map p8.
The Wine Council of Ontario,
Mississauga: 24–25, 32 (top rt),
34, 35, 86–87, 186–187.
The Wine Institute, San Francisco:
28 (both).